I JoY

3 STEP WRITING

Preview

1

Writing에 필요한 문법

해당 Unit의 영작을 위해 필요한 문법사항을
학습합니다.

2

Writing에 필요한 문법 확인

문제풀이를 통해 앞에서 배운 문법사항을
확인합니다.

3

Word List

해당 Unit의 영작을 위해 필요한
기본 단어를 익힙니다.

4

Step 1: 문장 시작하기

영작할 문장의 주어 또는 주어와 서술부의
일부를 써보며 문장을 시작합니다.

5

Step 2: 문장 만들기

동사 또는 수식어를 활용하여 Step 1에서
시작한 문장을 이어나갑니다.

6

Step 3: 문장 완성하기

수식어 또는 수식어구를 활용하여 Step 2에서
만든 기본 문장들을 완성합니다.

7

Quiz Time

해당 Lesson에서 학습한 단어와 문법사항을
복습하고 영작활동을 통해 이를 적용합니다.

8

Check Up

다양한 유형의 활동을 통해 해당 Unit에서
학습한 것을 확인합니다.

 영작을 위한 학생들의 이해도를
돕기 위해 간혹 어색한
한국말 표현이 있을 수 있음을
알려드립니다.

Contents

Unit 1

Lesson 1	can 긍정문	6
Lesson 2	can 부정문	14
Lesson 3	can 의문문	22

Unit 1. Check Up   30

Unit 2

Lesson 1	Should 긍정문과 부정문	32
Lesson 2	명령문	40
Lesson 3	제안문	48

Unit 2. Check Up   56

Unit 3

Lesson 1	have to 긍정문	58
Lesson 2	have to 부정문	66
Lesson 3	have to 의문문	74

Unit 3. Check Up 82

Unit 4

Lesson 1	현재완료 긍정문	84
Lesson 2	현재완료 부정문	92
Lesson 3	현재완료 의문문	100

Unit 4. Check Up 108

Answer Key 110

can 긍정문

Writing에 필요한 문법

① can 긍정문의 형태

주어	can	동사원형	
I			
You / We / They	can	eat	a lot.
He / She / It			

② can 긍정문 맛보기

STEP 1

나는	~할 수 있다
↓	↓
I	can

STEP 2

나는	점프할 수 있다
↓	↓
I	can jump

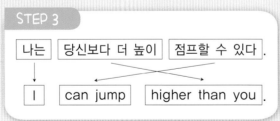

STEP 3

나는	당신보다 더 높이	점프할 수 있다	.
↓			
I	can jump	higher than you	.

③ can 긍정문의 쓰임

쓰임	예문	해석
능력을 표현	We can finish this tonight.	~할 수 있다
허락을 표현	You can go to the bathroom.	~해도 된다

* 비교급: 사람이나 사물을 비교할 때, 비교하는 대상 사이에 than을 사용한다

형용사 비교급	형용사 + -er	more + 형용사
예시	faster, taller, stronger 등	more beautiful, more interesting 등
예문	I can walk faster than you.	This movie is more interesting than that one.

Writing에 필요한 문법 확인

A. 다음 중 비교급이 있는 문장에 동그라미 하세요.

1 I can read faster than you.

2 This book is very interesting.

3 These flowers are more beautiful than those ones.

4 We can study together.

5 We can jump higher than them.

B. 다음 중 알맞은 것을 고르세요.

1 Mom can (speak / speaks) English well.

2 Jenny can (go / goes) now.

3 The dog can (eat / eats) the food.

4 We can (ask / asks) our teacher.

5 They can (run / runs) fast.

C. 다음 문장을 can 긍정문으로 바꿔 쓰세요.

1 My teacher speaks Japanese. _____

2 You take a nap. _____

3 John answers the question. _____

4 I ride a horse. _____

5 Cathy works fast. _____

D. 주어진 단어를 사용하여 문장을 완성하세요.

1 I / lift / can / the box / .

_____

2 can / you / hear / the birds / .

_____

3 Mom / make / lunch / can / .

_____

4 can / open / you / the windows / .

_____

5 help / can / we / the animals / .

_____

Word List

English	Korean	English	Korean
climb	오르다	move in	이사 오다
do	하다	park	공원
eat out	외식하다	speak	말하다
go on a picnic	소풍을 가다	top	정상, 꼭대기
Korean	한국어	walk	걷다

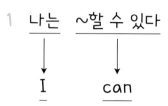 다음의 우리말 표현을 영어로 쓰세요.

1 나는   ~할 수 있다
          ↓   ↓
          I   can

2 Jenny는   ~할 수 있다

_____

3 그들은   ~할 수 있다

_____

4 Tanya는   ~할 수 있다

_____

5 우리는   ~할 수 있다

_____

6 Gina는   ~할 수 있다

_____

7 당신은   ~할 수 있다

_____

8 내 할아버지는   ~할 수 있다

_____

9 그들은   ~할 수 있다

_____

10 Jason은   ~할 수 있다

_____

 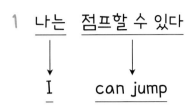 **다음의 우리말 표현을 영어로 쓰세요.**

1 나는 점프할 수 있다

   ↓   ↓

   I   can jump

2 Jenny는 달릴 수 있다

_____

3 그들은 외식할 수 있다

_____

4 Tanya는 말할 수 있다

_____

5 우리는 소풍갈 수 있다

_____

6 Gina는 (악기를) 연주할 수 있다 (play)

_____

7 당신은 이사올 수 있다

_____

8 내 할아버지는 걸을 수 있다

_____

9 그들은 오를 수 있다

_____

10 Jason은 할 수 있다 (do)

_____

 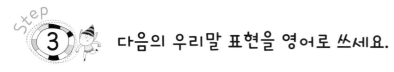 **다음의 우리말 표현을 영어로 쓰세요.**

1 나는 당신보다 더 높이 점프할 수 있다.

I can jump higher than you .

2 Jenny는 당신보다 더 빨리 달릴 수 있다.

_____

3 그들은 내일 (tomorrow) 외식할 수 있다.

_____

4 Tanya는 한국어를 말할 수 있다.

_____

5 우리는 공원에 (at the park) 소풍갈 수 있다.

_____

6 Gina는 피아노를 연주할 수 있다 .

_____

7 당신은 다음 달에 (next month) 이사올 수 있다.

_____

8 내 할아버지는 몇 시간 동안 (for a few hours) 걸을 수 있다.

_____

9 그들은 그 정상까지 (to the top) 오를 수 있다.

_____

10 Jason은 이것을 (this) 할 수 있다.

_____

A. 빈칸을 채우세요.

English	Korean	English	Korean
	오르다		이사 오다
do		park	
	외식하다	speak	
go on a picnic			정상, 꼭대기
Korean			걷다

B. 빈칸을 채우세요.

1 사람이나 사물을 비교할 때   을 사용한다.

2 I can walk   than you. (나는 당신보다 더 빨리 걸을 수 있다.)

3 This movie is   than that one.

(이 영화가 저 영화보다 더 흥미롭다.)

C. 다음 중 비교급에 동그라미 하세요.

1 My sister is taller than Jane.

2 This box is heavier than that one.

3 I am stronger than him.

D. 그림을 보고 can과 주어진 동사를 사용하여 문장을 완성하세요.

1

2

3

4

Word Box

watch　　　　ride　　　　swim　　　　play

1　The boy _____ in the sea.

2　The girl _____ a bike.

3　You _____ TV.

4　They _____ soccer after school.

can 부정문

Writing에 필요한 문법

① can 부정문의 형태

주어	cannot	동사원형	
I			
You / We / They	cannot (can't)	jump	high.
He / She / It			

② can 부정문 맛보기

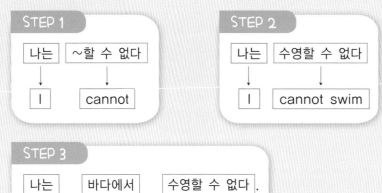

STEP 1

나는	~할 수 없다
↓	↓
I	cannot

STEP 2

나는	수영할 수 없다
↓	↓
I	cannot swim

STEP 3

나는	바다에서	수영할 수 없다 .
↓		
I	cannot swim	in the sea .

③ can 부정문의 쓰임

쓰임	예문	해석
능력을 표현	I can't climb that tree.	
상황을 표현	Dad can't cook tonight.	~할 수 없다
불허락, 불허가를 표현	You can't take a picture here.	

여기서  잠깐!

* can vs. may

	can	may
쓰임	주로 능력을 표현	주로 허락을 표현
해석	~할 수 있다	~해도 된다
예문	I can run for many hours. (나는 몇 시간 동안 뛸 수 있다.)	You may swim here. (당신은 여기서 수영을 해도 된다.)

can과 may 모두 허락의 뜻을 나타낼 수도 있으나 may의 경우는 좀 더 정중한 표현으로 사용된다.

Writing에 필요한 문법 확인

A. 다음 중 알맞은 것을 고르세요.

1 I cannot (study / studies) right now.

2 We can't (ride / rides) a bike here.

3 Dad cannot (fix / fixes) the blender.

4 Sean can't (join / joins) the party.

5 You can't just (disappear / disappears).

B. 주어진 단어를 사용하여 문장을 완성하세요.

1 You _____ TV. (may) (당신은 TV를 봐도 된다.)

2 Dad _____ home tonight. (cannot)
(아빠는 오늘 집에 올 수 없다.)

3 You _____ in. (may) (당신은 들어와도 된다.)

4 They _____ the windows now. (can)
(그들은 지금 창문을 열어도 된다.)

5 Your dog _____ here. (may)
(당신 개가 여기에서 놀아도 된다.)

C. 다음 문장을 부정문으로 바꿔 쓰세요.

1 Rob can eat all the food.   _____

2 I can move the desk.   _____

3 Sarah can speak Chinese.   _____

4 You can go home.   _____

5 We can go to the beach.   _____

D. 다음 문장을 can 부정문으로 바꿔 쓰세요.

1 You run around here.   _____

2 I study at nighttime.   _____

3 Eric gets up early.   _____

4 Mom reads for many hours.   _____

5 You take a short nap.   _____

Word List

English	Korean	English	Korean
buy	사다	go in	들어가다
cook	요리하다	sea	바다
disappear	사라지다	shower	샤워를 하다
far	(거리가) 먼	tonight	오늘 밤에, 오늘 밤
focus	집중하다	ticket	표, 티켓

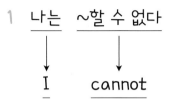 다음의 우리말 표현을 영어로 쓰세요.

1 나는   ~할 수 없다

   I   cannot

2 우리는   ~할 수 없다

_____

3 Cathy는   ~할 수 없다

_____

4 그들은   ~할 수 없다

_____

5 Tom은   ~할 수 없다

_____

6 나는   ~할 수 없다

_____

7 당신은   ~할 수 없다

_____

8 소들은 (cows)   ~할 수 없다

_____

9 엄마는 (Mom)   ~할 수 없다

_____

10 Sarah는   ~할 수 없다

_____

Step
2 다음의 우리말 표현을 영어로 쓰세요.

1 나는 수영할 수 없다

 ↓   ↓

 I   cannot swim

2 우리는 들어갈 수 없다

_____

3 Cathy는 걸을 수 없다

_____

4 그들은 집중할 수 없다

_____

5 Tom은 끝낼 수 없다 (finish)

_____

6 나는 샤워를 할 수 없다

_____

7 당신은 사라질 수 없다

_____

8 소들은 먹을 수 없다

_____

9 엄마는 요리할 수 없다

_____

10 Sarah는 살 수 없다

_____

 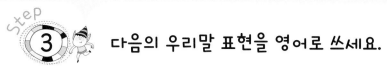 다음의 우리말 표현을 영어로 쓰세요.

1 나는 바다에서 수영할 수 없다.

   I cannot swim in the sea .

2 우리는 거기에 (there) 들어갈 수 없다.

   _____

3 Cathy는 그렇게 멀리까지 (that far) 걸을 수 없다.

   _____

4 그들은 지금 (right now) 집중할 수 없다.

   _____

5 Tom은 이 모든 것을 (all of this) 끝낼 수 없다.

   _____

6 나는 집에서 (in my house) 샤워를 할 수 없다.

   _____

7 당신은 단지 (just) 사라질 수 없다.

   _____

8 소들은 그 음식을 (the food) 먹을 수 없다.

   _____

9 엄마는 오늘 밤에 요리할 수 없다.

   _____

10 Sarah는 그 표를 (the ticket) 살 수 없다.

   _____

A. 빈칸을 채우세요.

English	Korean	English	Korean
	사다	go in	
	요리하다		바다
disappear		shower	
	(거리가) 먼		오늘 밤에, 오늘 밤
focus		ticket	

B. 빈칸을 채우세요.

_____	_____
주로 능력을 표현하며 '~할 수 있다' 로 해석	주로 허락을 표현하며 '~해도 된다' 로 해석
(예문) I _____ for many hours. (나는 몇 시간 동안 뛸 수 있다.)	(예문) You _____ here. (당신은 여기서 수영을 해도 된다.)
can과 may 모두 허락의 뜻을 나타낼 수도 있으나 _____의 경우는 좀 더 정중한 표현으로 사용된다.	

C. 그림을 보고 can과 주어진 동사를 사용하여 부정문을 완성하세요.

1

2

3

4

Word Box

join   run   go   ride

1 You ＿＿＿＿＿＿＿＿＿＿＿ a bike here.

2 We ＿＿＿＿＿＿＿＿＿＿＿ to the beach today.

3 Lily ＿＿＿＿＿＿＿＿＿＿＿ around here.

4 Sean ＿＿＿＿＿＿＿＿＿＿＿ the party.

can 의문문

Writing에 필요한 문법

① can 의문문의 형태

Can	주어	동사원형
Can	I	go?
	you / they / we	
	he / she / it	

② can 의문문 맛보기

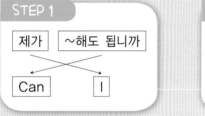

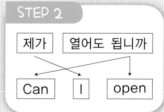

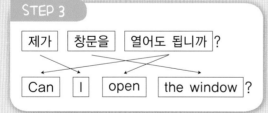

③ can 의문문의 쓰임

쓰임	예문	해석
능력과 상황에 대해 물어볼 때	Can you go there with me?	~할 수 있습니까?
물건을 살 때	Can I get two of the strawberry ice cream?	
허락을 구할 때	Can I use your ruler?	~해도 됩니까?

* can 의문문 대답

예문	긍정	부정
Can you get some bread for me? (당신은 나를 위해 빵을 좀 사다줄 수 있습니까?)	Yes, I can. Sure. Of course.	No, I can't. I'm sorry. I'm afraid not.
Can I go now? (저 지금 가도 됩니까?)	Yes, you can. Okay. Sure.	No, you can't. I'm afraid not. I'm sorry.
실생활에서는 can 의문문 대답으로 Yes의 의미로 'Sure.'이나 No의 의미로 'I'm sorry.' 등의 표현을 자주 사용한다.		

Writing에 필요한 문법 확인

A. 다음 중 알맞은 것을 고르세요.

1 Can you (make / makes) a sandcastle?

2 Mom, can I (play / plays) basketball?

3 Can they (fix / fixes) the door?

4 Can we (leave / leaves) early?

5 Can Gina (climb / climbs) to the top?

B. 다음 질문에 대한 대답을 완성하세요.

1 Can Jenny go to the park? Yes, _____.

2 Can they build a bridge? O_____.

3 Can Rob buy the ticket? No, _____.

4 Can you close the door? S _____.

5 Can I use your eraser? Yes, _____.

C. 다음 문장을 의문문으로 바꿔 쓰세요.

1 They can eat now. _____

2 We can go to the park. _____

3 You can wash your car. _____

4 I can do this. _____

5 Cathy can read the book. _____

D. 다음 중 틀린 부분을 바르게 고치세요.

1 Can you rides a bike? _____

2 Can they saw the movie? _____

3 Can his shower now? _____

4 Can we took a picture here? _____

5 Can I speaks to John? _____

Word List

English	Korean	English	Korean
beach	해변	open	열다
early	일찍	puppy	강아지
get	얻다, 가지다, 사다	stair	계단
get up	일어나다	take care of	~을/를 돌보다
Korean food	한국 음식	window	창문

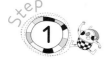 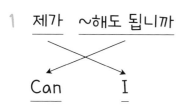 다음의 우리말 표현을 영어로 쓰세요.

1 제가 ~해도 됩니까

Can I

2 당신은 ~할 수 있습니까

_____

3 우리는 ~할 수 있습니까

_____

4 Aaron은 ~할 수 있습니까

_____

5 그들은 ~할 수 있습니까

_____

6 당신들은 ~할 수 있습니까

_____

7 Lisa는 ~할 수 있습니까

_____

8 제가 ~해도 됩니까

_____

9 당신은 ~할 수 있습니까

_____

10 당신의 토끼는 (your rabbit) ~할 수 있습니까

_____

 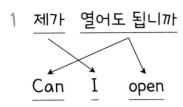 다음의 우리말 표현을 영어로 쓰세요.

1 제가 열어도 됩니까

Can I open

2 당신은 살 수 있습니까

_____

3 우리는 갈 수 있습니까

_____

4 Aaron은 탈 수 있습니까 (ride)

_____

5 그들은 만들 수 있습니까 (make)

_____

6 당신들은 일어날 수 있습니까

_____

7 Lisa는 돌볼 수 있습니까

_____

8 제가 놀아도 됩니까 (play)

_____

9 당신은 걸어 올라갈 수 있습니까 (walk up)

_____

10 당신의 토끼는 먹을 수 있습니까

_____

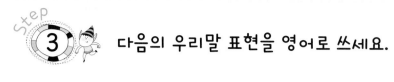

3 다음의 우리말 표현을 영어로 쓰세요.

1 제가 창문을 열어도 됩니까?

Can I open the window ?

2 당신은 약간의 우유를 (some milk) 살 수 있습니까?

_____

3 우리는 해변에 (to the beach) 갈 수 있습니까?

_____

4 Aaron은 자전거를 (a bike) 탈 수 있습니까?

_____

5 그들은 한국 음식을 만들 수 있습니까?

_____

6 당신들은 일찍 일어날 수 있습니까?

_____

7 Lisa는 그 강아지를 (the puppy) 돌볼 수 있습니까?

_____

8 제가 친구들과 함께 (with friends) 놀아도 됩니까?

_____

9 당신은 그 계단들을 (the stairs) 걸어 올라갈 수 있습니까?

_____

10 당신의 토끼는 많은 당근들을 (a lot of carrots) 먹을 수 있습니까?

_____

A. 빈칸을 채우세요.

English	Korean	English	Korean
beach			열다
	일찍	puppy	
get			계단
	일어나다	take care of	
Korean food			창문

B. 빈칸을 채우세요.

예문	긍정	부정
Can you get some bread for me? (당신은 나를 위해 빵을 좀 사다줄 수 있습 니까?)	Yes, I can. _____ Of course.	No, I can't. _____ I'm afraid not.
Can I go now? (저 지금 가도 됩니까?)	_____ Okay. Sure.	No, you can't. I'm afraid not. I'm sorry.

C. 그림을 보고 can과 주어진 단어를 사용하여 의문문과 대답을 완성하세요.

1

2

3

4

Word Box

close   go   fix   buy

1 _____ Eric _____ the ticket?   Yes, _____.

2 _____ Gina and Rob _____ to the park? No, _____.

3 _____ you _____ the door?   Of _____.

4 _____ you _____ the window?   S_____.

A. 주어진 단어를 사용하여 문장을 완성하세요.

make	speak	climb	open	lift

1 I _____ the heavy box.
(나는 그 무거운 상자를 들어올릴 수 없다.)

2 _____ you _____ the window?
(창문 좀 열어주시겠어요?)

3 Dad _____ dinner tonight.
(아빠가 오늘 저녁을 만들 수 있다.)

4 _____ Gina _____ Chinese?
(Gina는 중국어를 말할 수 있습니까?)

5 They _____ to the top.
(그들은 정상까지 올라갈 수 있다.)

B. 다음 중 비교급이 있는 문장에 동그라미 하세요.

1 I can read faster than you.

2 We can go home now.

3 I can jump higher than you.

4 They can study together.

5 This flower is more beautiful than that one.

C. 주어진 단어를 사용하여 문장을 완성하세요.

1 very well / the boy / play the guitar / can / .

_____

2 move in / next month / you / can't / .

_____

3 may / you / swim / here / .

_____

4 Lisa / can / take care of / the puppy / ?

_____

D. 다음 문장을 영작하세요.

1 우리가 그 불쌍한 동물들을 도울 수 있다. (the poor animals)

_____

2 제가 TV를 봐도 됩니까? (watch TV)

_____

3 나는 이 모든 것을 끝낼 수 없다. (all of this)

_____

4 Sarah는 그 표를 살 수 없다. (the ticket)

_____

should 긍정문과 부정문

Writing에 필요한 문법

① should 긍정문과 부정문의 형태

주어	should(긍정문)/should not(부정문)	동사원형
I		
You / They / We	should/ should not(shouldn't)	go out.
He / She / It		

② should 긍정문과 부정문 맛보기

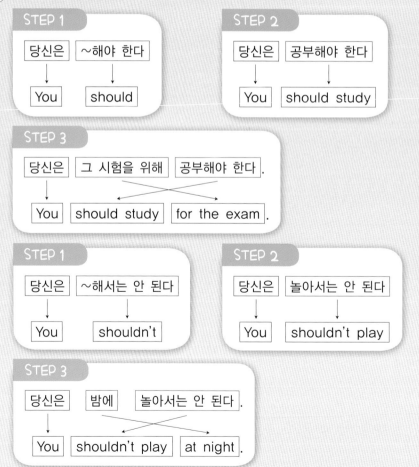

STEP 1

당신은	~해야 한다
↓	↓
You	should

STEP 2

당신은	공부해야 한다
↓	↓
You	should study

STEP 3

당신은	그 시험을 위해	공부해야 한다 .
↓		
You	should study	for the exam .

STEP 1

당신은	~해서는 안 된다
↓	↓
You	shouldn't

STEP 2

당신은	놀아서는 안 된다
↓	↓
You	shouldn't play

STEP 3

당신은	밤에	놀아서는 안 된다 .
↓		
You	shouldn't play	at night .

③ should 긍정문과 부정문의 쓰임

쓰임	예문	해석
조언이나 충고를 할 때	He should stay here tonight.	~해야 한다
	We shouldn't run in the classroom.	~해서는 안 된다

＊ some과 any
- some과 any는 '몇몇의, 약간의'라는 의미이다.
- some은 긍정문과 권유 및 요청에 종종 사용된다.
  (예문) I have some apples.   Do you want some water?
- any는 부정문과 의문문에 종종 사용된다.
  (예문) I don't have any books.
        (any는 부정문에서 '어떤'이라는 의미로 해석된다.)
  (예문) Did you bring any snacks?

Writing에 필요한 문법 확인

A. 다음 중 알맞은 것을 고르세요.

1 They have (some / any) milk. (그들은 약간의 우유를 가지고 있다.)

2 She doesn't have (some / any) money. (그녀는 어떤 돈도 가지고 있지 않다.)

3 I don't have (some / any) pencils. (나는 어떤 연필들도 가지고 있지 않다.)

4 The boy will buy (some / any) books. (그 소년은 몇몇의 책들을 살 것이다.)

B. some이나 any 중에서 알맞은 것을 쓰세요.

1 I will meet _____ friends. (나는 몇몇의 친구들을 만날 것이다.)

2 He didn't bring _____ food. (그는 어떤 음식도 가지고 오지 않았다.)

3 Can you give me _____ sugar? (당신은 나에게 약간의 설탕을 줄 수 있습니까?)

4 I don't have _____ paper. (나는 어떤 종이도 가지고 있지 않다.)

C. 다음 중 알맞은 것을 고르세요.

1 He (should / shoulds) plant trees on the mountain.

2 Jennifer should (buy / buys) some strawberries.

3 We should (eat not / not eat) too much chocolate.

4 You (should'nt / shouldn't) play outside in the rain.

5 They (not should / should not) be late for school.

D. Should와 Shouldn't를 사용하여 문장을 완성하세요.

1 You _____ run in a restaurant.

2 You _____ exercise every day.

3 You _____ help your friend.

4 You _____ wear a hat in the sun.

5 You _____ drive fast in the rain.

Word List

English	Korean	English	Korean
exercise	운동하다	subway	지하철
follow	따르다	sweets	단것들
listen	귀기울이다	throw away	버리다
rule	규칙	touch	만지다
save	저축하다	trash	쓰레기

 다음의 우리말 표현을 영어로 쓰세요.

1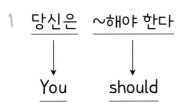
당신은 ~해야 한다
You   should

당신은 ~해서는 안 된다
You   shouldn't

2 우리는 ~해야 한다

_____

3 당신은 ~해서는 안 된다

_____

4 학생들은 (students) ~해야 한다

_____

5 아이들은 (kids) ~해서는 안 된다

_____

6 그들은 ~해야 한다

_____

7 당신은 ~해야 한다

_____

8 당신들은 ~해서는 안 된다

_____

9 우리는 ~해야 한다

_____

10 그 아기는 (the baby) ~해서는 안 된다

_____

 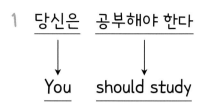 다음의 우리말 표현을 영어로 쓰세요.

1 당신은 공부해야 한다   당신은 놀아서는 안 된다

    ↓   ↓   ↓   ↓

   You   should study   You   shouldn't play

2 우리는 따라야 한다

   _____

3 당신은 버려서는 안 된다

   _____

4 학생들은 귀기울여야 한다

   _____

5 아이들은 먹어서는 안 된다 (eat)

   _____

6 그들은 타야 한다 (take)

   _____

7 당신은 운동해야 한다

   _____

8 당신들은 봐서는 안 된다

   _____

9 우리는 저축해야 한다

   _____

10 그 아기는 만져서는 안 된다

   _____

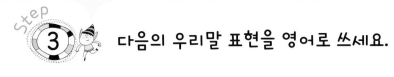

Step 3 다음의 우리말 표현을 영어로 쓰세요.

1 당신은 시험을 위해 공부해야 한다. 당신은 밤에 놀아서는 안 된다.
You should study for the exam . You shouldn't play at night .

2 우리는 그 규칙들을 (the rules) 따라야 한다.

_____

3 당신은 쓰레기를 버려서는 안 된다.

_____

4 학생들은 그들의 선생님에게 (to their teacher) 귀기울여야 한다.

_____

5 아이들은 너무 많은 단것들을 (too many sweets) 먹어서는 안 된다.

_____

6 그들은 지하철을 타야 한다.

_____

7 당신은 매일 (every day) 운동해야 한다.

_____

8 당신들은 TV를 봐서는 안 된다.

_____

9 우리는 돈을 (money) 저축해야 한다.

_____

10 그 아기는 그 뜨거운 그릇을 (the hot bowl) 만져서는 안 된다.

_____

A. 빈칸을 채우세요.

English	Korean	English	Korean
	운동하다	subway	
follow			단것들
	귀기울이다	throw away	
rule			만지다
save			쓰레기

B. 빈칸을 채우세요.

1 some과 any는 　　　　　 또는 　　　　　 라는 의미이다.

2 some은 　　　　　 과 권유 및 요청에 종종 사용된다.

3 any는 　　　　　 과 　　　　　 에 종종 사용된다.

any는 부정문에서 　　　　　 이라는 의미로 해석된다.

C. 다음 중 알맞은 것을 고르세요.

1 They didn't wash (some / any) vegetables.
(그들은 어떤 채소들도 씻지 않았다.)

2 He will make (some / any) cookies. (그는 약간의 쿠키들을 만들 것이다.)

3 Do you want (some / any) cake? (당신은 약간의 케이크를 원합니까?)

4 She doesn't have (some / any) water. (그녀는 어떤 물도 가지고 있지 않다.)

D. 그림을 보고 주어진 단어를 이용하여 충고하는 문장을 완성하세요.

1

2

3

4

Word Box

stop   go   go to bed   shout

1 We _____ at red lights.

2 She _____ late.

3 He _____ to the dentist.

4 You _____ in the classroom.

명령문

Writing에 필요한 문법

① 명령문의 형태

		동사원형	
긍정 명령문		Open	the door.
부정 명령문	Don't	open	

② 명령문 맛보기

STEP 1

청소해라
↓
Clean

STEP 2

당신의 방을 청소해라

Clean your room

STEP 3

당신의 방을 먼저 청소해라.

Clean your room first .

STEP 1

운전하지 마라
↓
Don't drive

STEP 2

빨리 운전하지 마라

Don't drive fast

STEP 3

눈 속에서 빨리 운전하지 마라.

Don't drive fast in the snow .

③ 명령문의 쓰임

쓰임	예문	해석
명령할 때	Get up early.	~해라
금지나 경고를 나타낼 때	Don't be late.	~하지 마라

	many	much	a lot
의미	많은		
쓰임	셀 수 있는 명사 앞에	셀 수 없는 명사 앞에	셀 수 있는 명사와 셀 수 없는 명사 앞에
예시	many books many kids	much water much time	a lot of pencils a lot of milk

Writing에 필요한 문법 확인

A. 다음 중 알맞은 것을 고르세요.

1 Don't drink (many / a lot of) coffee.

2 Do you have (many / much) pencils?

3 There are (many / much) birds in the sky.

4 (Many / A lot of) water is in the bottle.

5 She doesn't have (many / much) time today.

B. 다음 중 틀린 부분을 고쳐 바르게 쓰세요. 틀린 부분이 없다면 X 하세요.

1 Jack drinks many juice every day. _____

2 I have much books in my room. _____

3 Did you eat a lot of cookies? _____

4 Maria bought much bananas. _____

5 Does she have many dogs? _____

C. 다음 중 알맞은 것을 고르세요.

1 (Close / Closes) the window.

2 (Be / Is) quiet in the classroom.

3 (Don't / Not) swim here.

4 (Be / Don't) kind to your friends.

5 (Be / Don't) play soccer on the street.

D. 다음 문장을 명령문으로 바꿔 쓰세요.

1 You are happy.

_____

2 You are kind.

_____

3 You practice the piano every day.

_____

4 You study math hard.

_____

5 You don't close your eyes.

_____

Word List

English	Korean	English	Korean
basketball	농구	give	주다
brush	닦다	name	이름
deep	깊은	paper	종이
flute	플루트	tomorrow	내일
garden	정원	tooth	이, 치아

Step 1 다음의 우리말 표현을 영어로 쓰세요.

1 청소해라   운전하지 마라
           ↓   ↓
      Clean   Don't drive

2 닦아라

3 꺾지 마라 (pick)

4 참석해라 (join)

5 (운동 경기를) 해라

6 수영하지 마라

7 (악기를) 연주하지 마라

8 주어라

9 써라 (write)

10 만지지 마라 (touch)

Step 2 다음의 우리말 표현을 영어로 쓰세요.

1 <u>당신의 방을</u> <u>청소해라</u>   <u>빨리</u> <u>운전하지 마라</u>

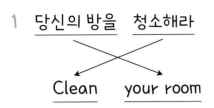   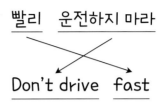

   <u>Clean</u> <u>your room</u>   <u>Don't drive</u> <u>fast</u>

2 당신의 이들을 (your teeth) 닦아라

_____

3 그 꽃들을 (the flowers) 꺾지 마라

_____

4 그 댄스 파티에 (the dance party) 참석해라

_____

5 농구를 해라

_____

6 강에서 (in the river) 수영하지 마라

_____

7 피아노를 (the piano) 연주하지 마라

_____

8 나에게 (me) 주어라

_____

9 당신의 이름을 써라

_____

10 그 수프를 (the soup) 만지지 마라

_____

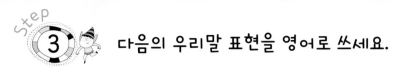

3 다음의 우리말 표현을 영어로 쓰세요.

1 당신의 방을 먼저 청소해라.   눈 속에서 빨리 운전하지 마라.

   Clean your room first .   Don't drive fast in the snow .

2 당신의 이들을 세 번 (three times) 닦아라.

   _____

3 정원에 있는 (in the garden) 그 꽃들을 꺾지 마라.

   _____

4 내일 그 댄스 파티에 참석해라.

   _____

5 방과 후에 (after school) 농구를 해라.

   _____

6 깊은 강에서 수영하지 마라.

   _____

7 밤에 (at night) 피아노를 연주하지 마라.

   _____

8 그 연필을 (the pencil) 나에게 주어라.

   _____

9 종이 위에 (on the paper) 당신의 이름을 써라.

   _____

10 그 뜨거운 (hot) 수프를 만지지 마라.

   _____

A. 빈칸을 채우세요.

English	Korean	English	Korean
basketball			주다
brush			이름
	깊은	paper	
flute			내일
	정원	tooth	

B. 빈칸을 채우세요.

1 many는 [　　　　] 명사 앞에 쓰인다.

2 much는 [　　　　] 명사 앞에 쓰인다.

3 a lot of는 [　　　　] 명사와 [　　　　] 명사 앞에 모두 쓰인다.

C. 다음 중 알맞은 것을 고르세요.

1 There are (many / much) computers in the classroom.

2 I ate (many / a lot of) soup in the morning.

3 She has (many / much) pencils.

4 Did you travel to (a lot of / much) countries?

5 He met (many / much) friends.

D. 그림을 보고 주어진 단어를 이용하여 명령문을 완성하세요.

1

2

3

4

Word Box

| wash | play | sit | help |

1 _____ outside today.

2 _____ your mother.

3 _____ down on the bench.

4 _____ your face.

제안문

① 제안문의 형태

		동사원형	
긍정 제안문	Let's	go	to the party.
부정 제안문	Let's not		

② 제안문 맛보기

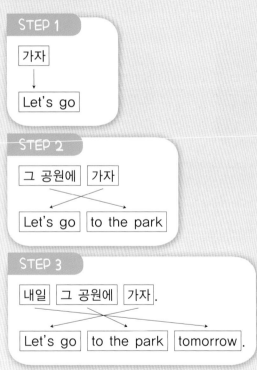

STEP 1

| 가자 |
| ↓ |
| Let's go |

STEP 2

| 그 공원에 | 가자 |
| Let's go | to the park |

STEP 3

| 내일 | 그 공원에 | 가자 . |
| Let's go | to the park | tomorrow . |

STEP 1

| 사지 말자 |
| ↓ |
| Let's not buy |

STEP 2

| 많은 것들을 | 사지 말자 |
| Let's not buy | many things |

STEP 3

| 너무 | 많은 것들을 | 사지 말자 . |
| Let's not buy | too | many things . |

③ 제안문의 쓰임

쓰임	예문	해석
상대방에게 제안할 때	Let's have dinner together.	~하자
	Let's not go to the party.	~하지 말자

＊ 최상급
– 셋 이상의 사람이나 사물을 비교할 때 사용하며 '가장 ~한'이라는 의미이다.
– 최상급 앞에는 the를 붙인다.
– 최상급 만드는 규칙

단어(형용사 또는 부사)	규칙	예시
대부분의 단어	단어 끝에 est를 붙인다.	fast – the fastest
-y로 끝나는 단어	y를 i로 고치고 est를 붙인다.	happy – the happiest
'한 개의 모음 + 한 개의 자음'으로 끝나는 단어	마지막 철자를 한 번 더 쓰고 est를 붙인다.	hot – the hottest
2음절 이상의 긴 단어	단어 앞에 the most를 붙인다.	beautiful – the most beautiful

Writing에 필요한 문법 확인

A. 주어진 단어의 최상급을 고르세요.

1 old (the older / the oldest)

2 pretty (prettiest / the prettiest)

3 big (the biggest / the bigest)

4 difficult (the most difficult / the difficultest)

B. 주어진 단어를 이용하여 빈칸에 최상급 표현을 쓰세요.

1 Tom is _____ student in his class. (tall)

2 Judy is _____ girl in her school. (pretty)

3 July is _____ month in Korea. (hot)

4 Math is _____ subject to me. (interesting)

C. 다음 문장을 제안문으로 바꿔 쓰세요.

1 We go fishing this Saturday.

_____

2 We don't play baseball there.

_____

3 We go to Sarah's birthday party.

_____

4 We don't pick the flowers.

_____

5 We have a good time.

_____

D. 주어진 단어를 사용하여 문장을 완성하세요.

1 meet / let's / at the park / them / .   _____

2 let's / dinner / have / together / .   _____

3 walk / tomorrow / let's not / to school / .   _____

4 speak / let's not / in the room / loudly / .   _____

5 go / for shoes / shopping / let's / .   _____

Word List

English	Korean	English	Korean
bring	가져오다	lunch	점심
climb	오르다	mountain	산
coke	콜라	ride	타다
hamburger	햄버거	Saturday	토요일
have	먹다	talk	말하다

 다음의 우리말 표현을 영어로 쓰세요.

1 가자
↓
Let's go

사지 말자
↓
Let's not buy

2 먹자

_____

3 하자 (do)

_____

4 만들자 (make)

_____

5 가져오자

_____

6 말하지 말자

_____

7 오르자

_____

8 타지 말자

_____

9 먹지 말자 (have)

_____

10 마시지 말자 (drink)

_____

1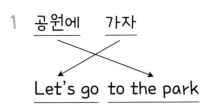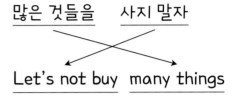

공원에   가자   많은 것들을   사지 말자

Let's go to the park   Let's not buy   many things

2   점심을   먹자

_____

3   우리의 숙제를 (our homework)   하자

_____

4   쿠키들을 (cookies)   만들자

_____

5   약간의 음식을 (some food)   가져오자

_____

6   크게 (loudly)   말하지 말자

_____

7   그 산을   오르자

_____

8   자전거를 (a bicycle)   타지 말자

_____

9   햄버거들을   먹지 말자

_____

10   콜라를   마시지 말자

_____

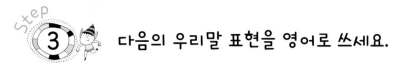

Step 3 다음의 우리말 표현을 영어로 쓰세요.

1 내일 공원에 가자.　　　　　너무 많은 것들을 사지 말자.

Let's go to the park tomorrow . Let's not buy too many things.

2 그 음식점에서 (at the restaurant) 점심을 먹자.

_____

3 방과 후에 (after school) 우리의 숙제를 하자.

_____

4 이번 토요일에 (this Saturday) 쿠키들을 만들자.

_____

5 그 파티에 (to the party) 약간의 음식을 가져오자.

_____

6 도서관에서 (in the library) 크게 말하지 말자.

_____

7 주말에 (on the weekend) 그 산을 오르자.

_____

8 길에서 (on the road) 자전거를 타지 말자.

_____

9 저녁으로 (for dinner) 햄버거들을 먹지 말자.

_____

10 너무 많은 (too much) 콜라를 마시지 말자.

_____

A. 빈칸을 채우세요.

English	Korean	English	Korean
	가져오다	lunch	
climb			산
	콜라	ride	
hamburger			토요일
	먹다	talk	

B. 빈칸을 채우세요.

1 최상급은 셋 이상의 사람이나 사물을 비교할 때 사용하며   이라는 의미이다.

2 최상급 앞에는   를 붙인다.

   – 최상급 만드는 규칙

단어 (형용사 또는 부사)	규칙
대부분의 단어	단어 끝에 를 붙인다.
-y로 끝나는 단어	y를 로 고치고 를 붙인다.
'한 개의 모음 + 한 개의 자음'으로 끝나는 단어	를 한 번 더 쓰고 를 붙인다.
2음절 이상의 긴 단어	단어 앞에 를 붙인다.

C. 그림을 보고 주어진 단어를 이용하여 제안문을 완성하세요.

1

2

3

4

Word Box

eat   swim   play   run

1 _____ sandwiches for breakfast.

2 _____ soccer after school.

3 _____ in the river.

4 _____ in the classroom.

A. 다음 중 알맞은 것을 고르세요.

1 Mr. Kim has (some / any) candies. (Mr. Kim은 약간의 사탕들을 가지고 있다.)

2 I don't have (some / any) coins. (나는 어떤 동전들도 가지고 있지 않다.)

3 Do you want (some / any) coffee? (당신은 약간의 커피를 원합니까?)

4 I don't like (some / any) toys. (나는 어떤 장난감들도 좋아하지 않는다.)

B. 틀린 부분을 찾아 바르게 고쳐 쓰세요. 틀린 부분이 없다면 X 하세요.

1 We have many rain in summer.

_____

2 Sam read much books last year.

_____

3 I usually bake a lot of bread on the weekend.

_____

4 My dad drinks a lot of coffee.

_____

C. 다음 중 알맞은 것을 고르세요.

1 Rebecca has (longer / the longest) hair in her class.

2 February is (shorter / the shortest) month of the year.

3 Math is (the most difficult / the difficultest) subject.

4 I am (the happyest / the happiest) girl in the world.

D. 주어진 단어를 사용하여 문장을 완성하세요.

1 He / eat / should not / sweets / .

_____

2 close / don't / the door / .

_____

3 at school / your friends / help / .

_____

4 not / the movie / watch / let's / .

_____

E. 다음 문장을 영작하세요.

1 우리는 그 방을 어지럽혀서는 안 된다. (should, mess up)

_____

2 빗속에서 당신의 비옷을 입어라. (wear, in the rain)

_____

3 내일 쇼핑을 가지 말자. (go shopping)

_____

4 방과 후에 당신의 숙제를 해라. (after school)

_____

Lesson 1

have to 긍정문

Writing에 필요한 문법

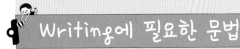

① have to 긍정문의 형태

주어	have to/has to	동사원형
I	have to	leave now.
You / They / We		
He / She / It	has to	

② have to 긍정문 맛보기

STEP 1

우리는	~해야 한다
↓	↓
We	have to

STEP 2

우리는	가야 한다
↓	↓
We	have to go

STEP 3

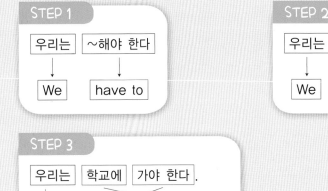

우리는	학교에	가야 한다	.

| We | have to go | to school |. |

③ have to 긍정문의 쓰임

쓰임	예문	해석
필요와 의무를 나타낼 때	She has to come home early.	~해야 한다

* 조동사 must 역시 '~ 해야 한다'라는 의미를 가지고 있지만, have to보다 더 강하게 어떤 일을
반드시 해야 한다는 어조를 나타낸다. (예문) You must fasten your seatbelt.

＊the가 쓰이는 곳

− 명사 앞에서 '그 ～'라는 뜻으로 쓰인다.

(예시) the book (그 책)　the girl (그 소녀)

− 서로 알고 있는 명사를 가리킬 때 쓰인다. 이 때는 '그 ～'라고 해석하지 않기도 한다.

(예문) Please open the window. (창문 좀 열어 주세요.)

− 앞에서 이미 언급되었던 것을 다시 말할 때 쓰인다.

(예문) I have a pencil. The pencil is long.

− 세상에서 유일한 자연 앞에 쓰인다.

(예시) the sun, the earth, the moon, the sky 등

− radio 앞에는 쓰이지만 TV 앞에는 쓰이지 않는다.

＊식사나 운동 경기 앞에 the를 쓰지 않는다

(예문) I have lunch.

We play baseball.

Writing에 필요한 문법 확인

A. 다음 중 알맞은 것을 고르세요.

1 (The / X) sun is hot.

2 I watched (the / X) TV yesterday.

3 We listen to (the / X) radio.

4 They will play (the / X) soccer tomorrow.

5 Did you have (the / X) dinner?

B. the가 들어갈 곳에 V 하세요. 필요 없다면 X 하세요.

1 John has breakfast at 8 o'clock.

2 Moon is bright.

3 We played tennis last weekend.

4 Can you close door?

5 There are many stars in sky.

C. 다음 중 알맞은 것을 고르세요.

1 He (have to / has to) do his homework.

2 I (have to / has to) clean my room.

3 Jane (have to / has to) go shopping today.

4 Mr. Kim has to (take / takes) an umbrella.

5 We (have to / has to) study hard for the exam.

D. 주어진 문장을 have to나 has to를 사용하여 다시 쓰세요.

1 You read this book.

_____

2 Sally goes there now.

_____

3 He works hard.

_____

4 I help my brother.

_____

5 My teacher sees a doctor.

_____

 Word List

English	Korean	English	Korean
answer	대답하다	practice	연습하다
come	오다	read	읽다
early	일찍	turn off	끄다
exercise	운동하다	visit	방문하다
get up	일어나다	wash	씻기다, 씻다

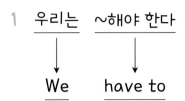 다음의 우리말 표현을 영어로 쓰세요.

1 우리는   ~해야 한다

   ↓   ↓

   We   have to

2 그녀는   ~해야 한다

   _____

3 당신은   ~해야 한다

   _____

4 Jason은   ~해야 한다

   _____

5 나는   ~해야 한다

   _____

6 그들은   ~해야 한다

   _____

7 Sally는   ~해야 한다

   _____

8 당신은   ~해야 한다

   _____

9 우리는   ~해야 한다

   _____

10 그는   ~해야 한다

   _____

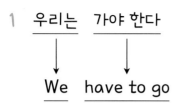

다음의 우리말 표현을 영어로 쓰세요.

1 우리는 가야 한다

   ↓   ↓

   We   have to go

2 그녀는 씻겨야 한다

   _____

3 당신은 일어나야 한다

   _____

4 Jason은 운동해야 한다

   _____

5 나는 읽어야 한다

   _____

6 그들은 와야 한다

   _____

7 Sally는 연습해야 한다

   _____

8 당신은 꺼야 한다

   _____

9 우리는 방문해야 한다

   _____

10 그는 대답해야 한다

   _____

Step 3 다음의 우리말 표현을 영어로 쓰세요.

1 우리는 학교에 가야 한다.

We have to go to school .

2 그녀는 그녀의 개를 (her dog) 씻겨야 한다.

_____

3 당신은 일찍 일어나야 한다.

_____

4 Jason은 그의 건강을 위해 (for his health) 운동해야 한다.

_____

5 나는 그 책을 (the book) 읽어야 한다.

_____

6 그들은 그 회의에 (to the meeting) 와야 한다.

_____

7 Sally는 바이올린을 (the violin) 연습해야 한다.

_____

8 당신은 라디오를 (the radio) 꺼야 한다.

_____

9 우리는 그녀의 집을 (her house) 방문해야 한다.

_____

10 그는 그 질문에 (the question) 대답해야 한다.

_____

A. 빈칸을 채우세요.

English	Korean	English	Korean
answer			연습하다
	오다	read	
early			끄다
	운동하다	visit	
get up			씻기다, 씻다

B. 빈칸을 채우세요.

*the가 쓰이는 곳

1 명사 앞에서 　　　　　라는 뜻으로 쓰인다.

2 서로 　　　　　명사를 가리킬 때 쓰인다.

3 앞에서 이미 　　　　　되었던 것을 다시 말할 때 쓰인다.

4 세상에서 　　　　　자연 앞에서 쓰인다.

5 식사나 　　　　　앞에는 the를 쓰지 않는다.

C. the가 바르게 쓰인 문장에 O, 잘못 쓰인 문장에 X 하세요.

1 Birds are flying in the sky.　　　　(　)

2 Did you play the baseball yesterday?　(　)

3 He opened the window.　　　　　(　)

4 I had the lunch with my friend.　　(　)

D. 그림을 보고 have to나 has to 및 주어진 동사를 이용하여 문장을 완성하세요.

1

2

3

4

Word Box

help   do   clean   practice

1 I _____ my homework.

2 He _____ the piano.

3 We _____ the old lady.

4 The girl _____ her room.

have to 부정문

1 have to 부정문의 형태

주어	don't have to/ doesn't have to	동사원형	
I	don't have to	run	fast.
You / They / We			
He / She / It	doesn't have to		

2 have to 부정문 맛보기

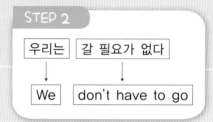

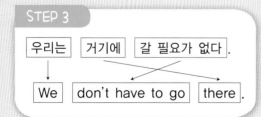

3 have to 부정문의 쓰임

쓰임	예문	해석
불필요함을 나타낼 때	She doesn't have to go to school on Sunday.	~할 필요가 없다

＊시간의 전치사 at, in, on
- 구체적이고 정확한 시간 앞에 at을 쓴다.
  (예문) I get up at 7 o'clock.
- 월, 계절, 연도 앞에 in을 쓴다.
  (예문) I will visit Canada in March.   She goes skiing in winter.
  He went there in 2017.
- 요일이나 날짜 앞에 on을 쓴다.
  (예문) We go to church on Sundays.   My birthday is on July 20.

Writing에 필요한 문법 확인

A. 빈칸에 알맞은 시간의 전치사를 쓰세요.

1 Her birthday is _____ March 15.

2 I have to get up _____ 8 o'clock.

3 Do you go swimming _____ summer?

4 Kelly visited England _____ 2016.

5 He will meet his friend _____ Friday.

B. 다음 중 틀린 부분을 고쳐 바르게 쓰세요. 틀린 부분이 없다면 X 하세요.

1 Bears sleep on winter.

_____

2 The party is at April 7.

_____

3 She makes cookies on Saturdays.

_____

4 I go to bed in 10 o'clock.

_____

C. 괄호 안의 단어가 들어갈 위치에 V 하세요.

1 You have to finish the work today. (don't)

2 She have to go to the meeting. (doesn't)

3 I have to buy a new jacket. (don't)

4 We don't cook dinner. (have to)

5 He doesn't buy the house. (have to)

D. 다음 문장을 부정문으로 바꿔 쓰세요.

1 You have to bring your lunch.

_____

2 He has to do his homework now.

_____

3 I have to fix the computer.

_____

4 Allen has to help her mother.

_____

5 They have to move the table.

_____

 **Word List**

English	Korean	English	Korean
clean	청소하다	raincoat	비옷
go to bed	잠자리에 들다	take	(교통수단을) 타다
early	일찍	tonight	오늘 밤에
library	도서관	wear	입다
plant	(나무나 꽃 등을) 심다	work	일하다

 다음의 우리말 표현을 영어로 쓰세요.

1 우리는   ～할 필요가 없다
   ↓   ↓
   We   don't have to

2 당신은   ～할 필요가 없다

_____

3 그는   ～할 필요가 없다

_____

4 우리는   ～할 필요가 없다

_____

5 Sunny는   ～할 필요가 없다

_____

6 나는   ～할 필요가 없다

_____

7 Alice는   ～할 필요가 없다

_____

8 그들은   ～할 필요가 없다

_____

9 우리는   ～할 필요가 없다

_____

10 그녀는   ～할 필요가 없다

_____

 **다음의 우리말 표현을 영어로 쓰세요.**

1 <u>우리는</u> <u>갈 필요가 없다</u>

     ↓   ↓

  <u>We</u> <u>don't have to go</u>

2 당신은 청소할 필요가 없다

_____

3 그는 갈 필요가 없다

_____

4 우리는 쉴을 필요가 없다

_____

5 Sunny는 잠자리에 들 필요가 없다

_____

6 나는 입을 필요가 없다

_____

7 Alice는 탈 필요가 없다

_____

8 그들은 조용히 할 필요가 없다 (be quiet)

_____

9 우리는 공부할 필요가 없다

_____

10 그녀는 일할 필요가 없다

_____

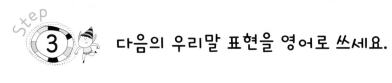

3 다음의 우리말 표현을 영어로 쓰세요.

1 우리는 거기에 갈 필요가 없다.

We don't have to go there .

2 당신은 당신의 집을 (your house) 청소할 필요가 없다.

_____

3 그는 도서관에 (to the library) 갈 필요가 없다.

_____

4 우리는 꽃들을 심을 필요가 없다.

_____

5 Sunny는 일찍 잠자리에 들 필요가 없다.

_____

6 나는 비옷을 입을 필요가 없다.

_____

7 Alice는 버스를 (a bus) 탈 필요가 없다.

_____

8 그들은 마당에서 (in the yard) 조용히 할 필요가 없다.

_____

9 우리는 오늘 밤에 공부할 필요가 없다.

_____

10 그녀는 일요일에 (on Sunday) 일할 필요가 없다.

_____

A. 빈칸을 채우세요.

English	Korean	English	Korean
clean			비옷
go to bed			(교통수단을) 타다
	일찍	tonight	
	도서관	wear	
plant			일하다

B. 빈칸을 채우세요.

1 구체적이고 정확한 시간 앞에 전치사 [   ]을 쓴다.

2 월, 계절, 연도 앞에 전치사 [   ]을 쓴다.

3 요일이나 날짜 앞에 전치사 [   ]을 쓴다.

C. 다음 중 알맞은 것을 고르세요.

1 I go to school (at / in / on) 9 o'clock.

2 He went to America (at / in / on) 2017.

3 Do you work (at / in / on) Saturday?

4 My mom's birthday is (at / in / on) May 20.

5 It rains a lot (at / in / on) July.

D. 그림을 보고 have to와 주어진 동사를 이용하여 부정문을 완성하세요.

1

2

3

4

Gina

Word Box

| get up | eat | paint | wash |

1　He _____ dinner now.

2　You _____ early today.

3　I _____ my car.

4　Gina _____ a picture.

Lesson 3

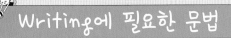

have to 의문문

Writing에 필요한 문법

① have to 의문문의 형태

Do/Does	주어	have to	동사원형	
Do	I			
	you / they / we	have to	stay	here?
Does	he / she / it			

② have to 의문문 맛보기

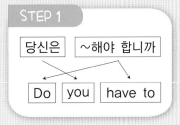

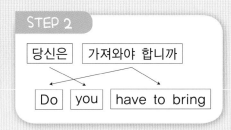

STEP 1

| 당신은 | ~해야 합니까 |

| Do | you | have to |

STEP 2

| 당신은 | 가져와야 합니까 |

| Do | you | have to bring |

STEP 3

| 당신은 | 그 책을 | 가져와야 합니까 |?

| Do | you | have to bring | the book |?

③ have to 의문문의 쓰임

예문	해석
Do they have to go to the museum?	~해야 합니까?
Does she have to make dinner?	

* have to 의문문에 대한 대답

- 긍정일 때는 'Yes, 주어 + have to / has to.'로 대답한다.
- 부정일 때는 'No, 주어 + don't have to / doesn't have to.'로 대답한다.
- 대답할 때의 주어에는 알맞은 대명사를 사용한다.
  (예문) Q: Does Jon have to walk to school?
  　　　A: Yes, he has to. / No, he doesn't have to.
  　　　Q: Do you have to learn Chinese?
  　　　A: Yes, I have to. / No, I don't have to.

Writing에 필요한 문법 확인

A. 알맞은 대답에 동그라미 하세요.

1 Q: Do I have to be quiet here?
　A: (Yes, I have to. / No, you don't have to.)

2 Q: Does my sister have to get up now?
　A: (Yes, she have to. / Yes, she has to.)

3 Q: Do you have to do the work?
　A: (No, I don't have to. / No, I doesn't have to.)

4 Q: Does Mark have to take a bus?
　A: (Yes, he have to. / No, he doesn't have to.)

B. 다음 질문에 대한 대답을 완성하세요.

1 Q: Do you have to wash your hands? 　　A: _____, I have to.

2 Q: Does she have to make dinner?
　A: _____, she doesn't have to.

3 Q: Do I have to do homework now? 　　A: No, _____.

4 Q: Does Tyler have to fix the computer? 　A: Yes, _____.

C. 주어진 단어를 사용하여 문장을 완성하세요.

1 have to / clean the house / you / do / ? _____

2 does / she / write a diary / have to / ? _____

3 drink milk / have to / do / I / ? _____

4 have to / does / join the party / Jeff / ? _____

5 do / go to work / they / have to / ? _____

D. 다음 문장을 의문문으로 바꿔 쓰세요.

1 She has to buy a gift for her brother.

_____

2 You have to see the doctor.

_____

3 I have to go to the bank.

_____

4 Mike has to come back home now.

_____

5 They have to be quiet in the library.

_____

Word List

English	Korean	English	Korean
bring	가져오다	learn	배우다
call	전화하다	science	과학
cow	소	speak	말하다
feed	먹이다	wait	기다리다
join	~에 가입하다	win	이기다

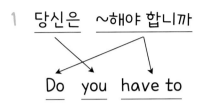 다음의 우리말 표현을 영어로 쓰세요.

1 <u>당신은</u> <u>~해야 합니까</u>

      <u>Do</u>   <u>you</u>   <u>have to</u>

2 우리는   ~해야 합니까

_____

3 Kevin은   ~해야 합니까

_____

4 그녀는   ~해야 합니까

_____

5 나는   ~해야 합니까

_____

6 그들은   ~해야 합니까

_____

7 그는   ~해야 합니까

_____

8 Maria는   ~해야 합니까

_____

9 Kelly와 Sarah는   ~해야 합니까

_____

10 Jay는   ~해야 합니까

_____

 다음의 우리말 표현을 영어로 쓰세요.

1 당신은 가져와야 합니까

   Do you have to bring

2 우리는 기다려야 합니까

   _____

3 Kevin은 이겨야 합니까

   _____

4 그녀는 말해야 합니까

   _____

5 나는 배워야 합니까

   _____

6 그들은 먹여야 합니까

   _____

7 그는 가입해야 합니까

   _____

8 Maria는 전화해야 합니까

   _____

9 Kelly와 Sarah는 청소해야 합니까 (clean)

   _____

10 Jay는 앉아야 합니까 (sit)

   _____

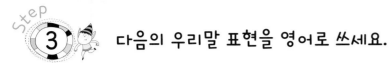

3 다음의 우리말 표현을 영어로 쓰세요.

1 당신은 그 책을 가져와야 합니까?

Do you have to bring the book ?

2 우리는 그를 (for him) 기다려야 합니까?

_____

3 Kevin은 그 게임을 (the game) 이겨야 합니까?

_____

4 그녀는 영어로 (in English) 말해야 합니까?

_____

5 나는 과학을 배워야 합니까?

_____

6 그들은 그 소들을 먹여야 합니까?

_____

7 그는 그 독서 모임에 (the book club) 가입해야 합니까?

_____

8 Maria는 그에게 (him) 전화해야 합니까?

_____

9 Kelly와 Sarah는 그 교실을 (the classroom) 청소해야 합니까?

_____

10 Jay는 여기에 (here) 앉아야 합니까?

_____

A. 빈칸을 채우세요.

English	Korean	English	Korean
	가져오다	learn	
call			과학
	소	speak	
feed			기다리다
	~에 가입하다	win	

B. 빈칸을 채우세요.

1 have to 의문문에 대한 긍정의 대답은 'Yes, 주어 + _____.'
로 답한다.

2 have to 의문문에 대한 부정의 대답은 'No, 주어 + _____.'
로 답한다.

C. 다음 질문에 대한 대답을 완성하세요.

Q: Dose Jack have to take the subway?   A: Yes, _____.

Q: Does your mom have to buy some food?   A: No, she _____.

D. 그림을 보고 have to와 주어진 동사를 사용하여 의문문을 완성하세요.

1

2

Jane

3

Tom

4

Word Box

write   study   go shopping   make

1 _____ they _____ a kite?

2 _____ Jane _____ today?

3 _____ Tom _____ a diary?

4 _____ you _____ math?

A. 빈칸에 the를 쓰세요. the가 필요 없다면 X 하세요.

1　Look at _____ sun!

2　They play _____ baseball every Saturday.

3　She has a computer. _____ computer is new.

4　Did you watch _____ TV last night?

B. 빈칸에 알맞은 전치사를 쓰세요.

1　Did you wake up _____ 6 o'clock?

2　My birthday is _____ May.

3　We go to church _____ Sundays.

4　Mr. Park went to Australia _____ 2015.

C. 다음 질문에 대한 대답을 완성하세요.

1　Q: Do you (당신) have to work now?
　　A: Yes, _____.

2　Q: Does Mark have to clean his room?
　　A: Yes, _____.

3　Q: Does your sister have to study now?
　　A: No, _____.

4　Q: Do you (당신들) have to leave tomorrow?
　　A: No, _____.

D. 주어진 단어를 사용하여 문장을 완성하세요.

1 have to / your homework / do / you / .

   _____

2 move / have to / Kelly / doesn't / the box / .

   _____

3 you / jog / have to / do / in the morning / ?

   _____

4 don't / you / wash / have to / the car / .

   _____

E. 다음 문장을 영작하세요.

1 당신은 밖에 나갈 필요가 없다. (have to, outside)

   _____

2 그녀는 그 모임에 갈 필요가 없다. (have to, to the meeting)

   _____

3 당신들은 집 한 채를 지어야 합니까? (have to, build)

   _____

4 나는 내 남동생을 돌보아야 한다. (have to, take care of)

   _____

현재완료 긍정문

Writing에 필요한 문법

① 현재완료 긍정문의 형태

주어에 따라 모양이 달라진다.

주어	have/has	동사의 과거분사 (p.p)	
I	have	lived	here for a long time.
You / They / We			
He / She / It	has		

② 현재완료 긍정문 맛보기

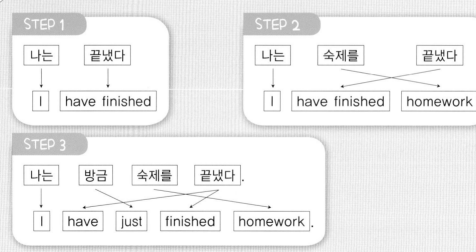

STEP 1

나는 끝냈다

I have finished

STEP 2

나는 숙제를 끝냈다

I have finished homework

STEP 3

나는 방금 숙제를 끝냈다 .

I have just finished homework .

③ 현재완료 긍정문의 쓰임

쓰임	예문	해석
과거에 시작해서 현재까지 계속 진행 중인 동작이나 상태를 표현	I have studied math for two hours.	~해 왔다
과거에 시작해서 방금 전에 완료된 동작을 표현	My dog has just finished her dinner.	~했다
경험해 본 일을 표현할 때	Justin has been to the museum.	~한 적이 있다

현재완료와 자주 함께 쓰이는 단어				
	for + 기간	since + 시점	just (방금)	already (벌써, 이미)
예문	My sister has studied Chinese for 10 months.	We've been together since 2015.	Dad has just fixed his car.	I've already finished homework.

Writing에 필요한 문법 확인

A. 다음 중 알맞은 것을 고르세요.

1 You (have / has) found a good house.

2 Mary (have / has) been a teacher for 10 years.

3 I (have / has) lived with my dog for 15 years.

4 Tom (have / has) been to the library.

5 We (have / has) used that computer for a long time.

B. 다음 중 알맞은 것을 고르세요.

1 I have played soccer (for / since) two hours.

2 Anne has known him (for / since) last year.

3 Aunt Gina has taught English (for / since) 2017.

4 Tony has lived in China (for / since) three years.

5 We have helped poor animals (for / since) many years.

C. 주어진 동사를 이용하여 문장을 완성하세요.

1 I have already _____ breakfast. (eat)

(나는 벌써 아침을 먹었다.)

2 Sean has just _____ pasta for Gina. (make)

(Sean은 방금 Gina를 위해 파스타를 만들었다.)

3 They have _____ that table for a long time. (have)

(그들은 그 탁자를 오랫동안 소유해 왔다.)

4 We have _____ the wall since yesterday. (paint)

(우리는 어제 이후로 그 벽에 페인트칠을 해 왔다.)

D. 다음 중 틀린 부분을 바르게 고쳐 현재완료 문장을 쓰세요.

1 You has been to Japan.

_____

2 Betty has study hard for the test.

_____

3 I have clean the house for one hour.

_____

4 They have see the show.

_____

 Word List

English	Korean	English	Korean
before	전에, 이전에	parent	부모
collect/collected	수집하다	rare	희귀한, 드문
elementary school	초등학교	science	과학
know/knew/known	알다	teach/taught	가르치다
live/lived	살다	Thai	태국의

Step 1  다음의 우리말 표현을 <u>현재완료를 사용하여</u> 영어로 쓰세요.

1 나는   끝냈다

    ↓   ↓

    <u>I</u> <u>have finished</u>

2 Ron은   살아왔다

  _____

3 당신은   공부해 왔다

  _____

4 우리는   가 본 적이 있다 (been to)

  _____

5 Jen은   먹어 봤다

  _____

6 그들은   알아 왔다

  _____

7 나는   수집해 왔다

  _____

8 Steve는   가르쳐 왔다

  _____

9 내 부모님들은 (my parents)   사용해 왔다 (used)

  _____

10 Sky는   본 적이 있다 (seen)

  _____

 다음의 우리말 표현을 <u>현재완료를 사용하여</u> 영어로 쓰세요.

1 나는   숙제를   끝냈다

   I have finished homework

2 Ron은 일본에서 (in Japan) 살아왔다

   _____

3 당신은 영어를 공부해 왔다

   _____

4 우리는 캐나다에 가 본 적이 있다

   _____

5 Jen은 그 음식을 (the food) 먹어 봤다

   _____

6 그들은 서로를 (each other) 알아 왔다

   _____

7 나는 책들을 (books) 수집해 왔다

   _____

8 Steve는 과학을 가르쳐 왔다

   _____

9 내 부모님들은 그 소파를 (the sofa) 사용해 왔다

   _____

10 Sky는 저 영화를 (that movie) 본 적이 있다

Step 3 다음의 우리말 표현을 <u>현재완료를 사용</u>하여 영어로 쓰세요.

1 나는 방금 숙제를 끝냈다.

I have just finished homework.

2 Ron은 일본에서 10년 동안 (for 10 years) 살아왔다.

_____

3 당신은 영어를 5년 동안 (for five years) 공부해 왔다.

_____

4 우리는 이미 (already) 캐나다에 가 본 적이 있다.

_____

5 Jen은 태국 음식을 (Thai food) 먹어 봤다.

_____

6 그들은 초등학교 이래로 (since elementary school) 서로를 알아 왔다.

_____

7 나는 희귀한 (rare) 책들을 수집해 왔다.

_____

8 Steve는 과학을 2년 동안 (for two years) 가르쳐 왔다.

_____

9 내 부모님들은 그 소파를 수년 동안 (for many years) 사용해 왔다.

_____

10 Sky는 전에 (before) 저 영화를 본 적이 있다.

_____

A. 빈칸을 채우세요.

English	Korean	English	Korean
	전에, 이전에	parent	
collect/collected			희귀한, 드문
elementary school			과학
	알다		가르치다
	살다	Thai	

B. 빈칸을 채우세요.

1 Dad has ⬜ fixed his car. (아빠가 방금 차를 고쳤다.)

2 I've ⬜ finished homework. (나는 이미 숙제를 끝냈다.)

3 My sister has studied Chinese ⬜ 10 months.

(내 여동생은 10개월 동안 중국어를 공부해 왔다.)

4 We have been together ⬜ 2015.

(우리는 2015년 이래로 함께 해 왔다.)

90

C. 그림을 보고 주어진 동사를 이용하여 현재완료 문장을 완성하세요.

1

2

3

4

Word Box

have   finish   make   help

1 Mom _____ pasta for me.

2 We _____ cleaning the house.

3 They _____ poor animals for a long time.

4 I _____ the table since 2015.

현재완료 부정문

① 현재완료 부정문의 형태

주어	have not / has not	동사의 과거분사 (p.p)	
I	have not(haven't)	finished	the work.
You / They / We			
He / She / It	has not(hasn't)		

② 현재완료 부정문 맛보기

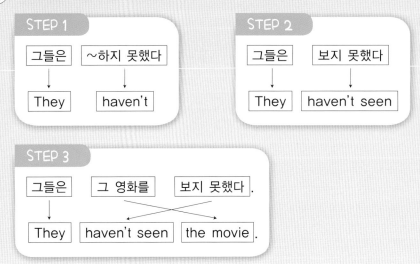

STEP 1

그들은	~하지 못했다
↓	↓
They	haven't

STEP 2

그들은	보지 못했다
↓	↓
They	haven't seen

STEP 3

그들은	그 영화를	보지 못했다.
They	haven't seen	the movie.

③ 현재완료 부정문의 쓰임

예문	해석
They haven't exercised since yesterday.	~하지 못했다, ~하지 않았다
Kevin hasn't been to the shop before.	~한 적이 없다

* yet(아직): 현재완료 부정문에 종종 사용된다

(예문) I haven't read the book yet. (나는 아직 그 책을 읽지 못했다.)

       We haven't decided yet. (우리는 아직 결정하지 못했다.)

* never: 현재완료 부정문에서 'not'을 대신해 쓸 수 있다

(예문) You have never been there. = You have not been there.

Writing에 필요한 문법 확인

A. 괄호 안의 단어가 들어갈 위치에 V 하세요.

1   He has been to New York. (not)

2   It has rained for three days. (not)

3   I have swum since my childhood. (not)

4   Jenny has visited her grandma since last April. (not)

5   They have worked since 3:00 p.m. (not)

B. 다음 중 알맞은 것을 고르세요.

1   You haven't packed (yet / already).

2   Dad has (yet / already) fixed the computer.

3   He has (just / yet) finished writing.

4   School hasn't started (just / yet).

5   We have (yet / already) worked so much.

C. 다음 중 틀린 부분을 바르게 고치세요.

1 I hasn't worked hard. _____

2 You haven't drive for a long time. _____

3 We haven't move the box yet. _____

4 They hasn't finished cleaning. _____

5 Mom haven't made dinner yet. _____

D. 다음 문장을 부정문으로 바꿔 쓰세요.

1 We have been to the restaurant. (not)

_____

2 Mom and Dad have painted the house. (never)

_____

3 Lily has just opened her shop. (not)

_____

4 I have made a cat toy. (never)

_____

5 Jenny has taught high school students. (not)

_____

Word List

English	Korean	English	Korean
build/built	만들다, 짓다	job	직업
cook/cooked	요리하다	meet/met	만나다
exercise/exercised	운동하다	prepare/prepared	준비하다
find/found	찾다, 발견하다	sandcastle	모래성
gym	체육관	take a shower/took a shower/taken a shower	샤워하다

 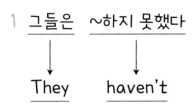 다음의 우리말 표현을 <u>현재완료를 사용하여</u> 영어로 쓰세요.

1 <u>그들은</u> <u>~하지 못했다</u>

   ↓   ↓

   <u>They</u>   <u>haven't</u>

2 우리는 ~하지 못했다

_____

3 Jessica는 ~하지 못했다

_____

4 당신은 ~한 적이 없다 (never)

_____

5 우리는 ~한 적이 없다

_____

6 그는 ~하지 못했다

_____

7 John은 ~하지 못했다

_____

8 Gina는 ~하지 않았다

_____

9 내 엄마는 (My mom) ~하지 않았다

_____

10 나는 ~하지 못했다

_____

 **2** 다음의 우리말 표현을 <u>현재완료를 사용하여</u> 영어로 쓰세요.

1 <u>그들은</u>   <u>보지 못했다</u>
   ↓   ↓
   <u>They</u>   <u>haven't seen</u>

2 우리는 가보지 못했다 (been to)

   _____

3 Jessica는 끝내지 못했다

   _____

4 당신은 만들어 본 적이 없다

   _____

5 우리는 만난 적이 없다

   _____

6 그는 찾지 못했다

   _____

7 John은 준비해 오지 못했다

   _____

8 Gina는 운동해 오지 않았다

   _____

9 엄마는 요리하지 않았다

   _____

10 나는 샤워를 하지 못했다

   _____

3 다음의 우리말 표현을 <u>현재완료를</u> 사용하여 영어로 <u>쓰세요</u>.

1 그들은 그 영화를 보지 못했다.

They haven't seen the movie .

2 우리는 프랑스에 (France) 가보지 못했다.

_____

3 Jessica는 그 프로젝트를 (the project) 끝내지 못했다.

_____

4 당신은 모래성을 (a sandcastle) 만들어 본 적이 없다.

_____

5 우리는 전에 (before) 만난 적이 없다.

_____

6 그는 직업을 (a job) 찾지 못했다.

_____

7 John은 시험을 대비해 (for the test) 준비해 오지 못했다.

_____

8 Gina는 그 체육관에서 (in the gym) 운동해 오지 않았다.

_____

9 엄마는 어제 이래로 (since yesterday) 요리하지 않았다.

_____

10 나는 아직 (yet) 샤워를 하지 못했다.

_____

A. 빈칸을 채우세요.

English	Korean	English	Korean
	만들다, 짓다		직업
cook/cooked		meet/met	
	운동하다		준비하다
	찾다, 발견하다	sandcastle	
gym			샤워하다

B. 빈칸을 채우세요.

1 yet(아직)은 　　　　　　에 종종 사용된다.

2 I haven't read the book 　　　　　. (나는 아직 그 책을 읽지 못했다.)

3 We haven't decided 　　　　　. (우리는 아직 결정하지 못했다.)

4 You have never been there. = You have 　　　　　 been there.

C. 그림을 보고 주어진 동사를 이용하여 현재완료 부정문을 완성하세요.

1

2

3

4

Word Box

make   swim   move   start

1 I _____ since last summer.

2 School _____ yet.

3 We _____ the box yet.

4 They _____ dinner yet.

현재완료 의문문

Writing에 필요한 문법

① 현재완료 의문문의 형태

Have/Has	주어	동사의 과거분사 (p.p)	
Have	I		
	you / they / we	made	it?
Has	he / she / it		

② 현재완료 의문문 맛보기

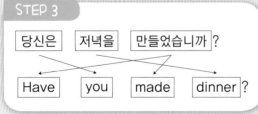

③ 현재완료 의문문의 쓰임

예문	해석
Has he had lunch?	~했습니까?
Have we been here before?	~한 적이 있습니까?
Has she studied French for many years?	~해 왔습니까?

＊ 현재완료 의문문에 대한 대답

예문	
질문	대답
Have you had breakfast?	Yes, I have. / No, I haven't.
Have they finished the project?	Yes, they have. / No, they haven't.
Have you(당신들) finished the project?	Yes, we have. / No, we haven't.
Has he fed the cats? Has she fed the cats?	Yes, he has. / No, he hasn't. Yes, she has. / No, she hasn't.

Writing에 필요한 문법 확인

A. 다음 중 알맞은 것을 고르세요.

1 (Have / Has) we worked hard?

2 (Have / Has) Gina already eaten the cookies?

3 (Have / Has) they been to the new mall?

4 (Have / Has) you emailed him?

5 (Have / Has) Rob taken a shower?

B. 다음 질문에 대한 대답을 완성하세요.

1 Have you exercised today?   Yes, _____.

2 Has Mina finished her homework?   Yes, _____.

3 Has Dad washed his car?   No, _____.

4 Have they cleaned the windows?   Yes, _____.

5 Has your cat slept since this morning? No, _____.

C. 주어진 동사를 이용하여 문장을 완성하세요.

1 Has the horse _____ well? (eat)

2 Have you _____ for the test? (prepare)

3 Have they ever _____ a tower? (build)

4 Has the boy _____ some milk? (get)

5 Have we _____ the fridge? (fix)

D. 다음 문장을 의문문으로 바꿔 쓰세요.

1 The girl has walked for many hours.

_____

2 They have lived in Korea for five years.

_____

3 Justin has won the race.

_____

4 We have seen that show before.

_____

5 You have been to the bakery.

_____

 **Word List**

English	Korean	English	Korean
arrive/arrived	도착하다	paint/painted	페인트칠을 하다, 칠하다
at home	집에	problem	문제
blender	믹서기	ride/rode/ridden	(말 등을) 타다
fix/fixed	고치다, 수리하다	wall	벽
leave/left	떠나다	water/watered	(식물 등에) 물을 주다

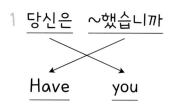 다음의 우리말 표현을 <u>현재완료</u>를 사용하여 영어로 쓰세요.

1 당신은 ～했습니까

  Have   you

2 Rob은 ～한 적이 있습니까

_____

3 그들은 ～했습니까

_____

4 Tom은 ～했습니까

_____

5 Hanna는 ～했습니까

_____

6 아빠는 ～했습니까

_____

7 당신은 ～했습니까

_____

8 나는 ～했습니까

_____

9 당신은 ～한 적이 있습니까

_____

10 우리는 ～한 적이 있습니까

_____

다음의 우리말 표현을 <u>현재완료를 사용하여</u> 영어로 쓰세요.

1 <u>당신은</u>　<u>만들었습니까</u>

<u>Have</u>　<u>you</u>　<u>made</u>

2 Rob은　가 본　적이 있습니까 (been to)

_____

3 그들은　칠했　습니까

_____

4 Tom은　떠났　습니까

_____

5 Hanna는　도착했　습니까

_____

6 아빠는　고쳤　습니까

_____

7 당신은　물을 주었　습니까

_____

8 제가　~을 했　습니까 (done)

_____

9 당신은　타 본　적이 있습니까

_____

10 우리가　가진　적이 있습니까 (had)

_____

3 다음의 우리말 표현을 <u>현재완료를 사용하여</u> 영어로 쓰세요.

1 당신은 저녁을 만들었습니까?

Have you made dinner ?

2 Rob은 일본에 (Japan) 가 본 적이 있습니까?

_____

3 그들은 그 벽을 (the wall) 칠했습니까?

_____

4 Tom은 학교로 (for school) 떠났습니까?

_____

5 Hanna는 집에 도착했습니까?

_____

6 아빠는 그 믹서기를 (the blender) 고쳤습니까?

_____

7 당신은 그 식물들에 (the plants) 물을 주었습니까?

_____

8 제가 어떤 잘못을 (something wrong) 했습니까?

_____

9 당신은 말을 (a horse) 타 본 적이 있습니까?

_____

10 우리가 이 문제를 (this problem) 가진 적이 있습니까?

_____

A. 빈칸을 채우세요.

English	Korean	English	Korean
	도착하다		페인트칠을 하다, 칠하다
	집에	problem	
blender			(말 등을) 타다
	고치다, 수리하다	wall	
leave/left			(식물 등에) 물을 주다

B. 빈칸을 채우세요.

1 Have you(당신) had breakfast?   Yes, _____ .

2 Have they finished the project?   No, _____ .

3 Has Eric fed his cats?   Yes, _____ .

4 Has Sarah been to Korea?   No, _____ .

C. 그림을 보고 주어진 단어를 사용하여 현재완료 의문문을 완성하세요.

1

2

3

Japanese
Rob

4

Justin

Word Box

clean   study   win   eat

1 _____ Gina already _____ the cookies?

2 _____ they _____ the windows?

3 _____ Rob _____ Japanese for many years?

4 _____ Justin _____ the race?

A. 주어진 동사를 이용하여 현재완료 문장을 완성하세요.

1 I _____ just _____ homework. (finish)
   (나는 숙제를 방금 끝냈다.)

2 My sister _____ Chinese for 10 months. (study)
   (내 누나는 10개월 동안 중국어를 공부해 왔다.)

3 Aunt Gina _____ English since 2017. (teach)
   (Gina 고모는 2017년 이래로 영어를 가르쳐 오고 있다.)

4 They _____ that table for a long time. (use)
   (그들은 저 탁자를 오랫동안 사용해 왔다.)

5 Justin _____ to the museum. (be)
   (Justin은 그 박물관에 가 본 적이 있다.)

B. 주어진 동사를 이용하여 현재완료 문장을 완성하세요.

1 They _____ the movie. (see)
   (그들은 그 영화를 본 적이 없다.)

2 School _____ yet. (start)
   (학교는 아직 시작하지 않았다.)

3 You _____ for a long time. (drive)
   (당신은 오랫동안 운전을 하지 않았다.)

4 Dad _____ dinner yet. (make)
   (아빠는 아직 저녁을 만들지 않았다.)

5 I _____ for the test. (prepare)
   (나는 그 시험을 준비하지 못했다.)

C. 다음 문장을 의문문으로 바꿔 쓰세요.

1 I have done something wrong.

_____

2 Mom has washed her car.

_____

3 The boy has got some milk.

_____

4 We have fixed the fridge.

_____

D. 다음을 현재완료 문장으로 영작하세요.

1 나는 희귀한 책들을 수집해 왔다. (collect, rare books)

_____

2 Kevin은 이전에 그 가게에 가 본 적이 없다. (the shop, before)

_____

3 그가 점심을 먹었습니까? (have lunch)

_____

4 당신들은 그 창문들을 닦았습니까? (clean the windows)

_____

Unit 1
Lesson 1 can 긍정문

Writing에 필요한 문법 확인

A. 1 I can read faster than you.
2 This book is very interesting.
3 These flowers are more beautiful than those ones.
4 We can study together.
5 We can jump higher than them.

B. 1 speak   2 go   3 eat   4 ask
5 run

C. 1 My teacher can speak Japanese.
2 You can take a nap.
3 John can answer the question.
4 I can ride a horse.
5 Cathy can work fast.

D. 1 I can lift the box.
2 You can hear the birds.
3 Mom can make lunch.
4 You can open the windows.
5 We can help the animals.

[Step 1]
2 Jenny can   3 They can
4 Tanya can   5 We can
6 Gina can   7 You can
8 My grandfather can
9 They can
10 Jason can

[Step 2]
2 Jenny can run
3 They can eat out
4 Tanya can speak
5 We can go on a picnic
6 Gina can play
7 You can move in
8 My grandfather can walk
9 They can climb
10 Jason can do

[Step 3]
2 Jenny can run faster than you .
3 They can eat out tomorrow .
4 Tanya can speak Korean .
5 We can go on a picnic at the park .
6 Gina can play the piano .
7 You can move in next month .
8 My grandfather can walk for a few hours .
9 They can climb to the top .
10 Jason can do this .

Unit 1. Lesson 1
Quiz Time

A.

English	Korean	English	Korean
climb	오르다	move in	이사 오다
do	~할 수 있다	park	공원
eat out	외식하다	speak	말하다
go on a picnic	소풍을 가다	top	정상, 꼭대기
Korean	한국어	walk	걷다

B. 1 비교급   2 faster
  3 more interesting
C. 1 My sister is ⟨taller⟩ than Jane.
  2 This box is ⟨heavier⟩ than that one.
  3 I am ⟨stronger⟩ than him.
D. 1 can swim   2 can ride
  3 can watch   4 can play

Unit 1
Lesson 2   can 부정문

◁ Writing에 필요한 문법 확인 ▷

A. 1 study   2 ride   3 fix   4 join
  5 disappear
B. 1 may watch   2 cannot come
  3 may come   4 can open
  5 may play
C. 1 Rob cannot(can't) eat all the
    food.
  2 I cannot(can't) move the desk.
  3 Sarah cannot(can't) speak
    Chinese.
  4 You cannot(can't) go home.
  5 We cannot(can't) go to the beach.
D. 1 You cannot(can't) run around here.
  2 I cannot(can't) study at nighttime.
  3 Eric cannot(can't) get up early.
  4 Mom cannot(can't) read for many
    hours.
  5 You cannot(can't) take a short
    nap.

[Step 1]
2 We cannot(can't)
3 Cathy cannot(can't)
4 They cannot(can't)
5 Tom cannot(can't)
6 I cannot(can't)
7 You cannot(can't)
8 Cows cannot(can't)
9 Mom cannot(can't)
10 Sarah cannot(can't)

[Step 2]
2 We cannot(can't) go in
3 Cathy cannot(can't) walk
4 They cannot(can't) focus
5 Tom cannot(can't) finish
6 I cannot(can't) shower
7 You cannot(can't) disappear
8 Cows cannot(can't) eat
9 Mom cannot(can't) cook
10 Sarah cannot(can't) buy

[Step 3]
2 We cannot(can't) go in there .
3 Cathy cannot(can't) walk that far .
4 They cannot(can't) focus right
  now .
5 Tom cannot(can't) finish all of this .
6 I cannot(can't) shower in my house .
7 You cannot(can't) just disappear.
8 Cows cannot(can't) eat the food .
9 Mom cannot(can't) cook tonight .

10 Sarah cannot(can't) buy the
ticket .

Unit 1. Lesson 2
Quiz Time

A.

English	Korean	English	Korean
buy	사다	go in	들어가다
cook	요리하다	sea	바다
disappear	사라지다	shower	샤워를 하다
far	(거리가) 먼	tonight	오늘 밤에, 오늘 밤
focus	집중하다	ticket	표, 티켓

B.

can	may
주로 능력을 표현하며 '~할 수 있다'로 해석	주로 허락을 표현하며 '~해도 된다'로 해석
(예문) I can run for many here. (나는 몇 시간 동안 뛸 수 있다.)	(예문) You may swim hours. (당신은 여기서 수영을 해도 된다.)
can과 may 모두 허락의 뜻을 나타낼 수도 있으나 may의 경우는 좀 더 정중한 표현으로 사용된다.	

C. 1 cannot(can't) ride
2 cannot(can't) go
3 cannot(can't) run
4 cannot(can't) join

Unit 1
Lesson 3 can 의문문

◀ Writing에 필요한 문법 확인 ▶

A. 1 make   2 play   3 fix   4 leave
5 climb
B. 1 Yes, she can.

2 Of course.
3 No, he can't.
4 Sure.
5 Yes, you can.
C. 1 Can they eat now?
2 Can we go to the park?
3 Can you wash your car?
4 Can I do this?
5 Can Cathy read the book?
D. 1 Can you ride a bike?
2 Can they see the movie?
3 Can he shower now?
4 Can we take a picture here?
5 Can I speak to John?

[Step 1]
2 Can you
3 Can we
4 Can Aaron
5 Can they
6 Can you
7 Can Lisa
8 Can I
9 Can you
10 Can your rabbit

[Step 2]
2 Can you get
3 Can we go
4 Can Aaron ride
5 Can they make
6 Can you get up
7 Can Lisa take care of
8 Can I play

112

9 Can you walk up

10 Can your rabbit eat

[Step 3]

2 Can you get some milk ?

3 Can we go to the beach ?

4 Can Aaron ride a bike ?

5 Can they make Korean food ?

6 Can you get up early ?

7 Can Lisa take care of the puppy ?

8 Can I play with friends ?

9 Can you walk up the stairs ?

10 Can your rabbit eat a lot of
   carrots ?

Unit 1. Lesson 3
Quiz Time

A.

English	Korean	English	Korean
beach	해변	open	열다
early	일찍	puppy	강아지
get	얻다, 가지다, 사다	stair	계단
get up	일어나다	take care of	~을/를 돌보다
Korean food	한국 음식	window	창문

B.

예문	긍정	부정
Can you get some bread for me? (당신은 나를 위해 빵을 좀 사다줄 수 있습니까?)	Yes, I can. Sure. Of course.	No, I can't. I'm sorry. I'm afraid not.
Can I go now? (저 지금 가도 됩니까?)	Yes, you can. Okay. Sure.	No, you can't. I'm afraid not. I'm sorry.

C. 1 Can, buy, he can

2 Can, go, they can't

3 Can, fix, course

4 Can, Sure

Unit 1. Check Up

A. 1 cannot(can't) lift   2 Can, open

3 can make   4 Can, speak

5 can climb

B. 1 I can read faster than you.

2 We can go home now.

3 I can jump higher than you.

4 They can study together.

5 This flower is more beautiful than that one.

C. 1 The boy can play the guitar very well.

2 You can't move in next month.

3 You may swim here.

4 Can Lisa take care of the puppy?

D. 1 We can help the poor animals.

2 Can I watch TV?

3 I cannot(can't) finish all of this.

4 Sarah cannot(can't) buy the ticket.

Unit 2

Lesson 1   Should 긍정문과 부정문

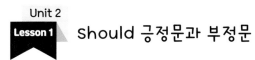

Writing에 필요한 문법 확인

A. 1 some   2 any   3 any   4 some

B. 1 some   2 any   3 some   4 any

C. 1 should   2 buy   3 not eat
   4 shouldn't   5 should not

D. 1 shouldn't   2 should   3 should
   4 should   5 shouldn't

[Step 1]

2 We should

3 You shouldn't

4 Students should

5 Kids shouldn't

6 They should

7 You should

8 You shouldn't

9 We should

10 The baby shouldn't

[Step 2]

2 We should follow

3 You shouldn't throw away

4 Students should listen

5 Kids shouldn't eat

6 They should take

7 You should exercise

8 You shouldn't watch

9 We should save

10 The baby shouldn't touch

[Step 3]

2 We should follow the rules .

3 You shouldn't throw away trash .

4 Students should listen to their
  teacher .

5 Kids shouldn't eat too many sweets .

6 They should take the subway .

7 You should exercise every day .

8 You shouldn't watch TV .

9 We should save money .

10 The baby shouldn't touch the hot
   bowl .

Unit 2. Lesson 1

Quiz Time

A.

English	Korean	English	Korean
exercise	운동하다	subway	지하철
follow	따르다	sweets	단것들
listen	귀기울이다	throw away	버리다
rule	규칙	touch	만지다
save	저축하다	trash	쓰레기

B. 1 몇몇의, 약간의
   2 긍정문
   3 부정문, 의문문, 어떤

C. 1 any   2 some   3 some   4 any

D. 1 should stop
   2 shouldn't go to bed
   3 should go
   4 shouldn't shout

Unit 2
Lesson 2 명령문

◁ Writing에 필요한 문법 확인 ▷

A. 1 a lot of   2 many   3 many
   4 A lot of   5 much

B. 1 Jack drinks much (a lot of) juice
   every day.

114

2 I have many (a lot of) books in my room.

3 X

4 Maria bought many (a lot of) bananas.

5 X

C. 1 Close   2 Be   3 Don't   4 Be

5 Don't

D. 1 Be happy.

2 Be kind.

3 Practice the piano every day.

4 Study math hard.

5 Don't close your eyes.

[Step 1]

2 Brush   3 Don't pick   4 Join

5 Play   6 Don't swim   7 Don't play

8 Give   9 Write   10 Don't touch

[Step 2]

2 Brush   your teeth

3 Don't pick   the flowers

4 Join   the dance party

5 Play   basketball

6 Don't swim   in the river

7 Don't play   the piano

8 Give   me

9 Write   your name

10 Don't touch   the soup

[Step 3]

2 Brush your teeth three times .

3 Don't pick the flowers in the
   garden .

4 Join the dance party tomorrow .

5 Play basketball after school .

6 Don't swim in the deep river.

7 Don't play the piano at night .

8 Give me the pencil .

9 Write your name on the paper .

10 Don't touch the hot soup.

Unit 2. Lesson 2

Quiz Time

A.

English	Korean	English	Korean
basketball	농구	give	주다
brush	닦다	name	이름
deep	깊은	paper	종이
flute	플루트	tomorrow	내일
garden	정원	tooth	이, 치아

B. 1 셀 수 있는

2 셀 수 없는

3 셀 수 있는, 셀 수 없는

C. 1 many   2 a lot of   3 many

4 a lot of   5 many

D. 1 Don't play   2 Help   3 Don't sit

4 Wash

Unit 2
Lesson 3   제안문

⟨ Writing에 필요한 문법 확인 ⟩

A. 1 the oldest

2 the prettiest

3 the biggest

4 the most difficult

Answer Key **115**

B. 1 the tallest

2 the prettiest

3 the hottest

4 the most interesting

C. 1 Let's go fishing this Saturday.

2 Let's not play baseball there.

3 Let's go to Sarah's birthday party.

4 Let's not pick the flowers.

5 Let's have a good time.

D. 1 Let's meet them at the park.

2 Let's have dinner together.

3 Let's not walk to school tomorrow.

4 Let's not speak loudly in the room.

5 Let's go shopping for shoes.

[Step 1]

2 Let's have

3 Let's do

4 Let's make

5 Let's bring

6 Let's not talk

7 Let's climb

8 Let's not ride

9 Let's not have

10 Let's not drink

[Step 2]

2 Let's have lunch

3 Let's do our homework

4 Let's make cookies

5 Let's bring some food

6 Let's not talk loudly

7 Let's climb the mountain

8 Let's not ride a bicycle

9 Let's not have hamburgers

10 Let's not drink coke

[Step 3]

2 Let's have lunch at the restaurant .

3 Let's do our homework after school .

4 Let's make cookies this Saturday .

5 Let's bring some food to the party .

6 Let's not talk loudly in the library .

7 Let's climb the mountain on the weekend .

8 Let's not ride a bicycle on the road .

9 Let's not have hamburgers for dinner .

10 Let's not drink too much coke.

Unit 2. Lesson 3

Quiz Time

A.

English	Korean	English	Korean
bring	가져오다	lunch	점심
climb	오르다	mountain	산
coke	콜라	ride	타다
hamburger	햄버거	Saturday	토요일
have	먹다	talk	말하다

B. 1 가장 ~한   2 the

단어 (형용사 또는 부사)	규칙
대부분의 단어	단어 끝에 est 를 붙인다.
-y로 끝나는 단어	y 를 i 로 고치고 est 를 붙인다.
'한 개의 모음 + 한 개의 자음'으로 끝나는 단어	마지막 철자 를 한 번 더 쓰고 est 를 붙인다.
2음절 이상의 긴 단어	단어 앞에 the most 를 붙인다.

C. 1 Let's eat

2 Let's play

3 Let's not swim

4 Let's not run

Unit 2. Check Up

A. 1 some 2 any 3 some 4 any

B. 1 We have much (a lot of) rain in summer.

2 Sam read many (a lot of) books last year.

3 X

4 X

C. 1 the longest

2 the shortest

3 the most difficult

4 the happiest

D. 1 He should not eat sweets.

2 Don't close the door.

3 Help your friends at school.

4 Let's not watch the movie.

E. 1 We shouldn't mess up the room.

2 Wear your raincoat in the rain.

3 Let's not go shopping tomorrow.

4 Do your homework after school.

Unit 3
Lesson 1 **have to 긍정문**

◀ Writing에 필요한 문법 확인 ▶

A. 1 The   2 X   3 the   4 X   5 X

B. 1 X

2 v Moon is bright.

3 X

4 Can you close v door?

5 There are many stars in v sky.

C. 1 has to   2 have to   3 has to

4 take   5 have to

D. 1 You have to read this book.

2 Sally has to go there now.

3 He has to work hard.

4 I have to help my brother.

5 My teacher has to see a doctor.

[Step 1]

2 She has to

3 You have to

4 Jason has to

5 I have to

6 They have to

7 Sally has to

8 You have to

9 We have to

10 He has to

[Step 2]

2 She has to wash

3 You have to get up

4 Jason has to exercise

5 I have to read

6 They have to come

7 Sally has to practice

8 You have to turn off

9 We have to visit

10 He has to answer

[Step 3]

2 She has to wash her dog .

3 You have to get up early .

4 Jason has to exercise for his
  health .

5 I have to read the book .

6 They have to come to the meeting .

7 Sally has to practice the violin .

8 You have to turn off the radio .

9 We have to visit her house .

10 He has to answer the question .

Unit 3. Lesson 1

Quiz Time

A.

English	Korean	English	Korean
answer	대답하다	practice	연습하다
come	오다	read	읽다
early	일찍	turn off	끄다
exercise	운동하다	visit	방문하다
get up	일어나다	wash	씻기다, 씻다

B. 1 그 ~   2 알고 있는   3 언급

  4 유일한   5 운동 경기

C. 1 (O)   2 (X)

  3 (O)   4 (X)

D. 1 have to do

  2 has to practice

  3 have to help

  4 has to clean

Unit 3
Lesson 2 have to 부정문

◀ Writing에 필요한 문법 확인 ▶

A. 1 on   2 at   3 in   4 in   5 on

B. 1 Bears sleep in winter.

  2 The party is on April 7.

  3 X

  4 I go to bed at 10 o'clock.

C. 1 You v have to finish the work
    today.

  2 She v have to go to the meeting.

  3 I v have to buy a new jacket.

  4 We don't v cook dinner.

  5 He doesn't v buy the house.

D. 1 You don't have to bring your lunch.

  2 He doesn't have to do his
    homework now.

  3 I don't have to fix the computer.

  4 Allen doesn't have to help her
    mother.

  5 They don't have to move the table.

[Step 1]

2 You don't have to

3 He doesn't have to

4 We don't have to

5 Sunny doesn't have to

6 I don't have to

7 Alice doesn't have to

8 They don't have to be

9 We don't have to

10 She doesn't have to

[Step 2]

2 You don't have to clean

3 He doesn't have to go

4 We don't have to plant

5 Sunny doesn't have to go to bed

6 I don't have to wear

7 Alice doesn't have to take

8 They don't have to be quiet

9 We don't have to study

10 She doesn't have to work

[Step 3]

2 You don't have to clean your house .

3 He doesn't have to go to the library .

4 We don't have to plant flowers .

5 Sunny doesn't have to go to bed early .

6 I don't have to wear a raincoat .

7 Alice doesn't have to take a bus .

8 They don't have to be quiet in the yard .

9 We don't have to study tonight .

10 She doesn't have to work on Sunday .

Unit 3. Lesson 2

Quiz Time

A.

English	Korean	English	Korean
clean	청소하다	raincoat	비옷
go to bed	잠자리에 들다	take	(교통수단을) 타다
early	일찍	tonight	오늘 밤에
library	도서관	wear	입다
plant	(나무나 꽃 등을) 심다	work	쓰다

B. 1 at   2 in   3 on

C. 1 at   2 in   3 on   4 on   5 in

D. 1 doesn't have to eat

2 don't have to get up

3 don't have to wash

4 doesn't have to paint

Unit 3
Lesson 3   have to 의문문

Writing에 필요한 문법 확인

A. 1 A: (Yes, I have to. / No, you don't have to.)

2 A: (Yes, she have to. / Yes, she has to.)

3 A: (No, I don't have to. / No, I doesn't have to.)

4 A: (Yes, he have to. / No, he doesn't have to.)

B. 1 Yes

2 No

3 you don't have to

4 he has to

C. 1 Do you have to clean the house?

2 Does she have to write a diary?

3 Do I have to drink milk?

4 Does Jeff have to join the party?

5 Do they have to go to work?

D. 1 Does she have to buy a gift for her brother?

2 Do you have to see the doctor?

3 Do I have to go to the bank?

4 Does Mike have to come back home now?

5 Do they have to be quiet in the library?

[Step 1]

2 Do we have to

3 Does Kevin have to

4 Does she have to

5 Do I have to

6 Do they have to

7 Does he have to

8 Does Maria have to

9 Do Kelly and Sarah have to

10 Does Jay have to

[Step 2]

2 Do we have to wait

3 Does Kevin have to win

4 Does she have to speak

5 Do I have to learn

6 Do they have to feed

7 Does he have to join

8 Does Maria have to call

9 Do Kelly and Sarah have to clean

10 Does Jay have to sit

[Step 3]

2 Do we have to wait for him ?

3 Does Kevin have to win the game ?

4 Does she have to speak in English ?

5 Do I have to learn science ?

6 Do they have to feed the cows ?

7 Does he have to join the book club ?

8 Does Maria have to call him ?

9 Do Kelly and Sarah have to clean the classroom ?

10 Does Jay have to sit here ?

Unit 3. Lesson 3

Quiz Time

A.

English	Korean	English	Korean
bring	가져오다	learn	배우다
call	전화하다	science	과학
cow	소	speak	말하다
feed	먹이다	wait	기다리다
join	~에 가입하다	win	이기다

B. 1 have to/has to

2 don't have to/doesn't have to

C. 1 he has to

2 doesn't have to

D. 1 Do, have to make

2 Does, have to go shopping

3 Does, have to write

4 Do, have to study

Unit 3. Check Up

A. 1 the   2 X   3 The   4 X

B. 1 at   2 in   3 on   4 in

C. 1 I have to

2 he has to

3 she doesn't have to

4 we don't have to

D. 1 You have to do your homework.

2 Kelly doesn't have to move the box.

3 Do you have to jog in the morning?

4 You don't have to wash the car.

E. 1 You don't have to go outside.

2 She doesn't have to go to the meeting.

3 Do you have to build a house?

4 I have to take care of my brother.

120

Unit 4
Lesson 1 현재완료 긍정문

⟨ **Writing에 필요한 문법 확인** ⟩

A. 1 have 2 has 3 have 4 has
  5 have

B. 1 for 2 since 3 since 4 for
  5 for

C. 1 eaten 2 made 3 had
  4 painted

D. 1 You have been to Japan.
  2 Betty has studied hard for the test.
  3 I have cleaned the house for one hour.
  4 They have seen the show.

[Step 1]

2 Ron has lived
3 You have studied
4 We have been to
5 Jen has eaten
6 They have known
7 I have collected
8 Steve has taught
9 My parents have used
10 Sky has seen

[Step 2]

2 Ron has lived in Japan
3 You have studied English
4 We have been to Canada
5 Jen has eaten the food

6 They have known each other
7 I have collected books
8 Steve has taught science
9 My parents have used the sofa
10 Sky has seen that movie

[Step 3]

2 Ron has lived in Japan for 10 years .
3 You have studied English for five years .
4 We have already been to Canada.
5 Jen has eaten Thai food.
6 They have known each other since elementary school .
7 I have collected rare books.
8 Steve has taught science for two years .
9 My parents have used the sofa for many years .
10 Sky has seen that movie before .

Unit 4. Lesson 1
Quiz Time

A.

English	Korean	English	Korean
before	전에, 이전에	parent	부모
collect/ collected	수집하다	rare	희귀한, 드문
elementary school	초등학교	science	과학
know/ knew/ known	알다	teach/ taught	가르치다
live/lived	살다	Thai	태국

B. 1 just
  2 already
  3 for

4 since

C. 1 has made

2 have finished

3 have helped

4 have had

Unit 4
Lesson 2 현재완료 부정문

Writing에 필요한 문법 확인

A. 1 He has ∨ been to New York.

2 It has ∨ rained for three days.

3 I have ∨ swum since my childhood.

4 Jenny has ∨ visited her grandma since last April.

5 They have ∨ worked since 3:00 p.m.

B. 1 yet   2 already   3 just   4 yet
5 already

C. 1 I haven't worked hard.

2 You haven't driven for a long time.

3 We haven't moved the box yet.

4 They haven't finished cleaning.

5 Mom hasn't made dinner yet.

D. 1 We have not(haven't) been to the restaurant.

2 Mom and Dad have never painted the house.

3 Lily has not(hasn't) just opened her shop.

4 I have never made a cat toy.

5 Jenny has not(hasn't) taught high school students.

[Step 1]

2 We haven't

3 Jessica hasn't

4 You have never

5 We haven't

6 He hasn't

7 John hasn't

8 Gina hasn't

9 My mom hasn't

10 I haven't

[Step 2]

2 We haven't been to

3 Jessica hasn't finished

4 You have never made

5 We haven't met

6 He hasn't found

7 John hasn't prepared

8 Gina hasn't exercised

9 My mom hasn't cooked

10 I haven't taken a shower

[Step 3]

2 We haven't been to France .

3 Jessica hasn't finished the project .

4 You have never made a sandcastle .

5 We haven't met before .

6 He hasn't found a job .

7 John hasn't prepared for the test .

8 Gina hasn't exercised in the gym .

9 My mom hasn't cooked since yesterday .

10 I haven't taken a shower yet .

Unit 4. Lesson 2

Quiz Time

A.

English	Korean	English	Korean
build/built	만들다, 짓다	job	직업
cook/cooked	요리하다	meet/met	만나다
exercise/exercised	운동하다	prepare/prepared	준비하다
find/found	찾다, 발견하다	sandcastle	모래성
gym	체육관	take a shower/took a shower/taken a shower	샤워하다

B. 1 현재완료 부정문

2 yet

3 yet

4 not

C. 1 haven't swum

2 hasn't started

3 haven't moved

4 haven't made

Unit 4

Lesson 3 현재완료 의문문

◀ Writing에 필요한 문법 확인 ▶

A. 1 Have 2 Has 3 Have 4 Have

5 Has

B. 1 I have 2 she has 3 he hasn't

4 they have 5 he/she hasn't

C. 1 eaten 2 prepared 3 built

4 got/gotten 5 fixed

D. 1 Has the girl walked for many hours?

2 Have they lived in Korea for five years?

3 Has Justin won the race?

4 Have we seen that show before?

5 Have you been to the bakery?

[Step 1]

2 Has Rob

3 Have they

4 Has Tom

5 Has Hanna

6 Has Dad

7 Have you

8 Have I

9 Have you

10 Have we

[Step 2]

2 Has Rob been to

3 Have they painted

4 Has Tom left

5 Has Hanna arrived

6 Has Dad fixed

7 Have you watered

8 Have I done

9 Have you ridden

10 Have we had

[Step 3]

2 Has Rob been to Japan ?

3 Have they painted the wall ?

4 Has Tom left for school ?

5 Has Hanna arrived at home ?

6 Has Dad fixed the blender ?

7 Have you watered the plants ?

8 Have I done something wrong ?

9 Have you ridden a horse ?

10 Have we had this problem ?

Unit 4. Lesson 3

Quiz Time

A.

English	Korean	English	Korean
arrive/ arrived	도착하다	paint/ painted	페인트칠을 하다, 칠하다
at home	집에	problem	문제
blender	믹서기	ride/rode/ ridden	(말 등을) 타다
fix/fixed	고치다, 수리하다	wall	벽
leave/ left	떠나다	water/ watered	(식물 등에) 물을 주다

B. 1 I have

2 they haven't

3 he has

4 she hasn't

C. 1 Has, eaten

2 Have, cleaned

3 Has, studied

4 Has, won

Unit 4. Check Up

A. 1 have, finished

2 has studied

3 has taught

4 have used

5 has been

B. 1 have not(haven't) seen

2 has not(hasn't) started

3 have not(haven't) driven

4 has not(hasn't) made

5 have not(haven't) prepared

C. 1 Have I done something wrong?

2 Has Mom washed her car?

3 Has the boy got some milk?

4 Have we fixed the fridge?

D. 1 I have collected rare books.

2 Kevin has not(hasn't) been to the shop before.

3 Has he had lunch?

4 Have you cleaned the windows?